THE ESSENTIAL KODAVA COOKBOOK

C. B. Muthamma was born in Kodagu in 1924. She graduated from Women's Christian College, Chennai. She was the first woman to join the Civil Service through the Union Public Service and went on to become India's first career woman ambassador. She lives in Delhi.

*

P. Gangamma Bopanna is an active social worker. She lives in Bangalore with her husband and children.

Best wishes.
C B Muthamma

THE ESSENTIAL KODAVA COOKBOOK

C.B. Muthamma

and

P. Gangamma Bopanna

PENGUIN BOOKS

Penguin Books India (P) Ltd., 11 Community Centre, Panchsheel Park, New Delhi 110 017, India
Penguin Books Ltd., 27 Wrights Lane, London W8 5TZ, UK
Penguin Putnam Inc., 375 Hudson Street, New York, NY 10014, USA
Penguin Books Australia Ltd., Ringwood, Victoria, Australia
Penguin Books Canada Ltd., 10 Alcorn Avenue, Suite 300, Toronto, Ontario M4V 3B2, Canada
Penguin Books (NZ) Ltd., Cnr Rosedale & Airborne Roads, Albany, Auckland, New Zealand

First published by Penguin Books India 2000

Series Editor: Bhicoo J. Manekshaw

10 9 8 7 6 5 4 3 2 1

Typeset in Sabon by Digital Technologies and Printing Solutions, New Delhi

Printed at Chaman Offset Printers, Delhi

Contents

Acknowledgements

Unstinting help and cooperation were received from Mrs K. Lalitha Devaiah who, to the deep sorrow of her friends, passed away very suddenly early in 1998.

Valuable help and cooperation were also received from Mrs C. Accavva Ganapathy and Mrs C. Vimala Iyyappa.

Acknowledgements

[illegible]

Foreword

C.B. Muthamma and P. Gangamma Bopanna are Kodava ladies who were brought up in Kodagu (Coorg) in traditional Kodava families. They are familiar with Kodava cuisine as also the customs and traditions of their community.

Miss Muthamma did her schooling in Kodagu and graduated from the Women's Christian College, Madras. She was the first woman to join the Civil Service after passing the Union Public Service Commission Examination and opted for the Foreign Service. She went on to become India's first career woman ambassador. She was a member of the Palme Commission on Disarmament and Security Issues, which presented its report to the United Nations Organization. After thirty-three years in the Foreign Service, she retired in 1982.

Mrs P. Gangamma Bopanna is an active social worker. She qualified as a lawyer, but married and raised a family, which took her away from the legal profession.

This tiny community of the Kodavas has distinguished itself in many fields. Independent India's first Chief of

Army Staff, Field Marshal Cariappa, was a Kodava.

Kodava food, customs and cooking utensils are unusual. This book makes fascinating reading and the recipes are worth trying out.

I hope you enjoy this book as much as we enjoyed working on it.

Bhicoo Manekshaw
Series Editor

Introduction

Kodagu (anglicised to Coorg) is a small region located on the Western Ghats touching Kerala on the south west. It has been a district of Karnataka State since 1956. The British had taken over Kodagu in 1834 from its erstwhile rulers. During the British period it was a Chief Commissioner's province, after which in the initial years of Independence it was a 'C' class state, with its own legislature, Council of Ministers and a Chief Secretary. Kodagu is the smallest district of Karnataka stretching sixty miles from north to south and about forty miles from east to west. Barring the capital region of Bangalore, it is the richest district in the state. Area for area, it is one of the richest agricultural regions of India, with a surplus in a variety of valuable crops. Rice was traditionally the staple crop, but the old system of mixed farming is still largely in existence. It includes growing fruit such as oranges and a variety of fine quality bananas, along with other items like coconut and areca nut. The important plantation crops include cardamom, coffee and pepper.

In the past, extensive forest areas dominated the Kodagu landscape but have been dwindling in recent decades. Out of these forests came valuable timber such as teak, rosewood, and other less well known varieties of wood, as also a range of jungle products like bamboo and good quality honey. These jungles were home to a rich variety of flora and fauna which had existed practically undisturbed until about a century ago. The animals included tiger, panther, bear, elephant, deer, wild pig, Indian bison, wild dog, jackal, porcupine and several others. But as the forests continue to shrink, the animal population has also diminished.

During the colonial period teak plantations were set up in the jungles to systematize its production.

Kodagu is watered by the south-west monsoon and gets heavy rains between June and August, with a few showers during the north-east monsoon in October and November. The river Kaveri flows through Kodagu, and is sacred to the Kodavas as well as the Hindus. Several other smaller streams and rivers flow through the region. Most of Kodagu is located 3000-4000 feet above sea level, and has a pleasant climate.

Apart from being fertile, Kodagu is beautiful hill country, lush and green, with terraced rice fields, orchards and plantations. The rice fields run between the hills like rivers, and in fact, in the Kodava language one talks of the 'shores' of rice fields. The terraces are narrow and steep in the higher zones but broaden out in the lower areas. Despite its small size Kodagu has a distinct identity, not only geographically and physically, but culturally as well. Its ethos is undoubtedly influenced by its geography and economy but above all by the various indigenous and other communities which have lived there harmoniously for centuries.

The Kodavas (Coorgs) are the people of this land. Although they bear the name of the land, they are only one of the many communities inhabiting the area. Many of them are indigenous, but several others have migrated to Kodagu over a period, from surrounding areas. The Kodavas are in fact a minority of the population, well under a quarter of the total inhabitants. The total population of Kodavas, both in and outside Kodagu has been estimated at about seventy or eighty thousand. People who have written about the Kodavas hold the view that they are an immigrant people. This view is based on the fact that they appear different from other communities of South India and have distinctive religious and social traditions. However, the origin of the Kodavas is a matter of conjecture, and there are many theories on the subject. Some maintain that they came from distant parts of northern India, and others that they came from outside India with one or more of the several waves of immigrations or conquests that took place over the centuries. They gradually worked their way to the south and to Kodagu which became their permanent home.

The history of the Kodavas does not seem to go back very far. The Kodava language has no script and there are no written records. There are only incidental references to the Kodavas in the histories of the wars and conquests of the region. The earliest references pertain to about seven or eight centuries ago. Such references usually occur in the context of the fairly frequent wars of territorial conquest by kings and chieftains of the region, and generally refer to them as being the fighting forces. In more recent history, during the invasions of Kodagu by the rulers of Mysore, or in the wars that resulted in the take-over of Kodagu by the British, the Kodavas are clearly established as the fighting forces of the rulers. These rulers however have almost always been from outside Kodagu. The indigenous non-Kodavas appear to have had, on the whole, a low profile.

The oral traditions of the Kodavas, including their folk legends, family lore or the various songs that accompany the ceremonies of births, marriages and death, throw no light on their past history. The strongest of the legends links them to the Kaveri Purana, the legend of the river goddess, Kaveri, who is the presiding deity of Kodagu, revered as the divine patron of Kodagu and the Kodavas. This, however, is not historical evidence.

There are accounts of the Kodavas in the colonial period by British administrators who had dealt with the area. These portray a community which was distinctly different in appearance, bearing, religion and customs, from other people within Kodagu and the surrounding regions. There are also references to the Kodavas being fiercely independent and self-confident, with no tendency to obsequiousness even towards their rulers.

The Kodavas were a people of farm and forest where the border between the two was, until recently, notional or non-existent. Even upto the early part of the twentieth century it was not unknown for farm cattle to be carried away by tigers, or for crops to be under threat by deer or monkeys. In fact, it was normal for the farmer to supplement the food from his farm with venison, wild pig, wild fowl, or yams and various green produce from the forest, along with fish from streams, ponds and his own rice fields.

The Kodavas have always been a martial people. This could be because of the environment in which they lived or due to inherited tradition. Guns and weaponry were part of the normal household items and in one of their principle festivals weapons are worshipped. This is followed by hunts in the forests. Although the hunts have now been discarded under the conservation laws, guns are still fired at births and deaths. In the past a man who killed a tiger celebrated this with a function called nari mangala, or 'tiger wedding'. He was thereafter entitled to grow sideburns as a mark of his feat.

During the takeover of Kodagu by the British it was agreed that the Kodavas would be entitled to keep guns. That facility still exists. Physical courage, prowess and good marksmanship have traditionally been much respected in the area. Even in modern times, with the younger generations leaving the land and branching out into other professions, a noticeable proportion of the youth still opt for the Armed Forces or the Forest Services. The first Indian Chief of Army Staff was a Kodava, Field Marshal K.M. Cariappa. He was followed a few years later as Chief of Army Staff by another Kodava, General K.S. Thimmayya, who had earlier held high-profile international peace keeping assignments.

*

Traditionally, Kodava society was organized in clans. All members of a given clan were related through the male line and claimed descent from a common founding ancestor. No one could marry within the same clan. The founding ancestor, called the kaarana, had a dominant role in the life and religion of the Kodavas. The kaarana and other ancestors were worshipped and prayers and offerings were made to them routinely, and on special occasions. In their core beliefs and rituals, the Kodavas were and still are ancestor worshippers. There are no caste or class distinctions within the community and every Kodava has a strong sense of personal dignity. There are no priests within the community. Moreover, non-Kodava priests have no role in core ceremonies relating to births, deaths and weddings.

Apart from ancestor worship in the family or clan, the farming communities have local village deities and temples, and prayers are offered there on designated occasions. Some aspects of Hinduism have also been assimilated, first in respect to goddess Kaveri, the holy river which rises in Kodagu, and second, in respect to Saivite beliefs and practices apparently acquired from the Saivite Rajas of Kodagu. There are Saivite temples across the border in Kerala venerated by the Kodavas. Though no priests are present during funerals or the following ceremonies, on the eleventh day after death, the bereaved go up to the Kaveri temple where non-Kodava priests preside, and Hindu rites are performed for the dead.

A striking feature of traditional Kodava society and the touchstone of its egalitarian and democratic philosophy was the position of the woman. Her role and rights mark out the Kodavas from most Indian communities. The woman had clearly recognized rights, whether in her natal or in her husband's home. There were no child marriages and the prospective bride and groom had a say in whom they were going to marry.

The status of the woman in the community did not depend on her marital status as in many traditional societies. If a woman remained unmarried, she had a claim to a share in the family property. The share of an unmarried woman was less than that of her brothers. The obvious reason for this was that she would only need to support herself whereas her brothers would have to support their families. After her death her share of the property reverted to the family. A married woman had no share in her natal family property, since she had her rights in her husband's family.

A married woman's links with her natal family were never severed, and were maintained in many ways. In earlier times, when the joint family was a reality and agriculture was more or less the sole occupation, a married woman was entitled to a ten-day break, called paththolivo, every year, in her natal home. In her husband's home she was busy all year round, managing the household and helping with the farm work. During these ten days she was in her own home, free of the constraints she would feel in the home of her in-laws. During that period she was not allowed to do even the most ordinary chores, but was pampered and looked after by her parents, brothers and sisters-in-law.

When a married daughter was expecting a baby, after the sixth or seventh month of pregnancy, members of her natal family would visit her husband's home and cook a festive lunch comprising of her favourite dishes, the ingredients for which they brought with them. After lunch they would take their daughter back with them for her confinement and for an additional period of a couple of months after the birth of the child, until she had recuperated. Thereafter, she and her baby were escorted back to her husband's home by members of her own family. This was done for the first two confinements.

In case of a woman's death, the natal family is still closely associated with the ceremonies and brings specified food and other items for the occasion. Even if any other member of her family dies—her husband or any of her children—the natal family responds in the same fashion. For the burial or cremation (both are practiced amongst the Kodavas) the natal family brings a rice flour preparation—usually a rice roti, and a fried egg, which are packed in a banana leaf. This is called koopadi (food packed for a journey). The custom is comparable to tribal practices elsewhere, and is probably meant to provision the departed on his or her last journey. However, it is not known why these two particular items are prepared. The packet is usually buried or cremated with the body. As modern crematoria do not permit inclusion of any extra item, koopadi is usually unwrapped and placed under a tree in the vicinity, so that birds or beasts eat it.

For the eleventh day ceremonies, called maada, the natal family sends a hamper filled with uncooked rice, coconuts, bananas, jaggery and betel leaves. The hamper is sent with a trusted servant who has to carry it on his head without putting it down until he reaches his destination. In the old days this usually meant that the man had to trudge through different villages, fields, and forests. In recognition of his effort, the hostess at the receiving end put oil on his head, to soothe it after carrying the burden. The contents of the hamper are used in the preparation of the day's meal for the family and guests participating in the maada. The jaggery and coconut are used in the green bean or mung dal paayasa which is invariably prepared only for the maada. This is never prepared at any other time in a Kodava home.

The daughter is entitled to be cremated, or buried in her family's burial ground. In the Kodava language there is a special word for a married woman's natal family—taamane. The English translation fails to give the importance and strength of this term and the honour that is attached by Kodava society in general and the married woman in particular to this concept and the traditions it stands for. The protection given by the taamane to a married woman is also extended to her children. Her children, like herself, have a claim to be buried or cremated in their mother's natal family burial ground. The children have a close link with, and many rights and claims on the mother's natal family. There have been cases when a married woman with young children died, her natal family took away the children and brought them up until they were grown up and even arranged their marriages. These customs still prevail.

On auspicious occasions like weddings, after the official public ceremony which is held separately in the homes of the bride and groom, after the lunch is over and the guests depart, a special baalé birudu or baalé maryadé is performed in honour of the natal clan of the mother of the bride or bridegroom. Three or five banana trunks are erected in an appropriate spot and the guests from the mother's natal family are invited to accept the honour. A male member performs a small ceremony during which a coconut is broken, the banana trunks are circumambulated and he then cuts each banana trunk with one stroke of his odi kathi (a large heavy unsheathed knife which forms part of traditional Kodava costume, fixed to the waistband at the back). The baalé birudu or baalé maryadé is a special tribute or honour given to very special parties on very special occasions, as when the bridegroom and his party go to the bride's home for the marriage ceremony.

During a wedding, the bride's maternal uncle's wife has the right to be her matron of honour. If there is no such person, a married cousin from the mother's natal clan is chosen. This and other traditions were symbols of the strong bonds between a married woman and her natal clan, and the high respect and importance accorded institutionally in Kodava society to a married woman's natal family.

Of particular interest from many points of view, is the wedding ceremony.

The actual wedding is traditionally a private function. The groom and his party go to the bride's home in the evening. For this function, members of the two families, the elders of both clans and senior people of related clans are present. There is no priest and no religious ceremony. The wedding is a civil contract in which the two sides make commitments in the presence of important people from both clans.

The representative and spokesman for the bride, being a person of standing, called the aruva, having first established his status and claim to speak, addresses the groom. He says, that the bride, until this moment, was their child and their daughter, but is now about to enter the groom's house as a woman and a wife. He demands to know what the groom is giving her. There is no question of a dowry. There is no dowry in Kodava society. Instead, the bridegroom has to confer certain rights to the bride, as the wife is a blessing upon the husband and his home, and it is up to him to be worthy of her. In the hearing of the assembled company, the bridegroom has to confer on his new bride rights over his home, land and other property. All he asks in return is that in the event of his wife leaving him for trifling reasons, who, in her natal family takes the responsibility of giving her good advice and sending her back to him. This refers to the fact that the wife, like the husband, has the right of divorce and remarriage. To this the bride's aruva responds that he gives this guarantee. He, in turn asks, that should their daughter encounter harsh treatment or harsh conditions in her husband's home and leaves him for good and sufficient reasons, who, on the husband's side, would guarantee that she would be sent home to her natal family with due respect and dignity, with an escort and a torch to light the way (Kodagu being jungle country). This guarantee is given by the groom's aruva and thereafter the ceremony proceeds and the wedding is completed.

The bride's aruva then ties to the end of the her sari eleven kallus or pebbles symbolizing gold coins in witness of her newly acquired rights in her husband's home. He keeps one pebble as a sign that this stands for the rights she retains in her natal clan, whose help and support she will always have. This ceremony which forms the core of Kodava weddings is called kallumbara adakuvo.

The reverse of this ceremony is held if there is a divorce, when the pebbles are taken back and the wedding pact is broken. It is called the kallumbara kaipo ceremony. A woman who is divorced or widowed has the right to remarry if she so chooses.

After the wedding the groom takes his new bride to his home. There is a ceremony in which the bride's trousseau, her jewellery and other items are shown to the guests assembled in the groom's home. This is because, should the bride leave the husband's home and family either because of a divorce or because of widowhood and re-marriage, everything she brought with her has to be returned. The husband and his family have no claim over these items. She could bring with her, property, bedding and other household items, especially a plate-cum-salver called a baakéthaliya (the bridal salver) which is used on most ceremonial occasions and also for everyday use. The idea underlying this is that the bride does not go empty-handed to her new home.

Apart from the central contractual features of a wedding, the peripherals are colourful. On the day preceeding the actual public and private functions, songs are sung by a male member of the clan to the accompaniment of a drum called dudi. These are traditional songs in praise of the two families. There is a charming song which describes the groom's prosperity, but his need of a wife to give him a home and children. The song describes him travelling around the land looking for a bride. When he comes to the particular house where his future bride lives, the parents, siblings and all other members of the family are providentially out on various errands. So the young daughter of the house does the usual honours due to a guest, offering him the customary pot of water at the entrance of the house to wash his feet and refresh himself. Whereupon the young man says, "If the hands that offer me this pot of water will always offer me a pot of water to welcome me, I will accept it". She then offers him refreshments which he also accepts with the same refrain, and so on, until the girl's parents are home and the happy accord is arrived at.

In actual fact, the older family members on the two sides negotiate the alliance with the concurrence of the two young people, the initial proposal having come from the groom's side. The Kodava community being a small one and Kodagu being a small compact area, most people in effect knew, or knew of each other, and were able to decide whether or not a particular alliance was acceptable. The agreement was formalized by a party of the groom's relatives who brought a ring for the bride—modrapana beppo.

There were other ceremonies immediately preceding the wedding, such as the henna ceremony for the bride, and the special wearing of bangles, as also the barber ceremony for the groom.

For the wedding ceremony (and on all other important occasions) the men and women on both sides wear full formal costume. For the men it is a black tunic reaching below the knees, with a red and gold waistband and white and gold turban. Apart from the odi kathi, the groom also carries a peecha kathi (a smaller knife) in a jewelled scabbard on the right side at the front. The women wear the Kodava style sari with pleats at the back, long sleeved blouses, scarves reaching below the knees at the back, and gold braid round the head. Traditional or other jewellery is worn on such occasions.

The bride and groom wear distinctive costumes. The groom wears a white tunic with full length sleeves, (the black tunic has sleeves stopping above the elbow) and carries a long staff. It is said, that in the past, in times of war if the groom had to fight on the battlefield or could not personally attend for other reasons, his staff stood in his place and the wedding ceremony continued. (One hopes of course, that the bridegroom returned from the battlefield.) The bride wears a red and gold sari with traditional jewellery, including on the top of her hands and feet. Instead of a scarf she wears a red and gold veil.

During various points in the festivities, the band which is in attendance strikes up and there is dancing, generally by the younger men; but sometimes young girls also join the dancing crowd. During the wedding the groom is attended by his best man and the bride by her matron of honour.

The bride and groom have a ceremonial bath on the morning of the wedding. They come in procession for the formal public ceremony and are led to a decorated dais and seated on a traditional three-legged stool called a mukkalı. A lighted brass lamp is placed near by. On another mukkali, a salver is placed along with uncooked rice and a small spouted container called kindi containing milk. The guests first put a few grains of rice on the head of the bride or groom, offer a sip of milk, and then give a gift of money. This ceremony is repeated at the private function which is the actual wedding, when the groom goes to the bride's home. The rice and milk are symbolic of prosperity and good fortune.

When the bride enters the groom's home, her new status as a wife is marked by a Ganga puja whereby she ceremonially fetches water and carries a small pot on her head, symbolizing that she is assuming her duties as wife. After the bride has assumed her position in her husband's home, she visits her natal home and formally makes offerings or meedi to her ancestors.

The ceremony of Ganga puja is also performed when she returns to her husband's home after childbirth. Here the ceremony symbolizes her resuming of household duties.

There was a custom whereby, in a family with no male heirs, a daughter could marry, and still retain her own clan name. Children born of the marriage would have their mother's clan name and have property rights in the mother's family, with no rights in the father's family property. It was called kuthik nippo i.e., ensuring the continuance of the family. The arrangement could be of two kinds—one in which the husband is committed entirely to his wife and family, or alternatively, one in which he is allowed a second wife whose children would have rights to his family property.

The emerging picture of the very strong position enjoyed traditionally by the Kodava woman was not just theoretical. She was brought up to be independent, self reliant and capable. She was not kept secluded or confined to the house. If a woman was widowed at a young age she proved herself capable of managing her affairs, looking after her husband's property and bringing up her children.

Kodava society was built on a great tradition of solidarity, effective in concentric circles. The innermost circle was the family, thereafter the clan, followed by other clans inhabiting the village called ooru karas along with the various other village communities. These communities provided common services as a matter of acknowledged right. For instance, the village washerman had the right to spread a carpet of white cloth on which the bride or bridegroom walked in procession to sit ceremonially on the dais. He was in turn entitled to special payment for the service. The landless farm workers or poleyas who lived on land allotted to them on the farm, played the band at weddings and other functions.

Before the establishment of schools, the rural communities had what was called kaisambala matha—whereby a qualified man, usually a Brahmin, was appointed to teach the children of the community to read and write. The payment for these and for most other services (including regular farm work) was usually in kind.

The ooru karas, families and clans, considered fellow villagers living in scattered farmsteads as important. They were involved in all occasions like marriages and deaths. During weddings which lasted for several days people of the village played a crucial role. One of the days preceding the wedding was designated as the day when the ooru karas gathered. On arrival they were met by the host family at the head of the lane or ani, leading to the house and given a ceremonial welcome with a band followed by a reception. Thereafter, during the wedding, they had to assume functions like the other members of the family. After the conclusion of the wedding, they were given a ceremonial farewell, again, with a band in attendance and the hosts accompanying them to the end of the lane.

At all functions, whether weddings, naming ceremonies or deaths, it was customary, for all guests to offer gifts of money, which, obviously, was useful in defraying expenses. Clan members also brought gifts in kind that were specifically used at that particular function, as for instance, unstitched white cloth at a funeral, required for various purposes including distribution to people doing menial jobs, or grain and jaggery required for the ceremony, etc.

On the actual day of the funeral no food is cooked in the house. Vegetarian food is brought in by close relations, neighbours and friends for the bereaved family and guests who come to pay their respects. In the house of death, until the eleventh day ceremonies are over, only vegetarian food is cooked, and no sweets or other delicacies are served.

Many of these customs are still intact, as they are still relevant, specially the money gifts, neighbours bringing food to the house of death as also the avoidance of non-vegetarian food for eleven days.

Some institutions like that of the leading clan assuming administrative and judicial roles in the community have long since been discarded. The dispute-settling mechanisms within family and clans are also gradually disappearing.

*

Kodagu is a land of heavy monsoons and the houses were

sturdily built. They were usually on a raised plinth, both because of the dampness and to keep away wild animals. The old clan headquarters, to which all the members of a clan had a right, were broadly of two types—the otheparè where the houses were constructed roughly in a straight line, or a house with all the rooms and facilities built round a quadrangle called a mundu. Both had a broad verandah running the length of the front, bound by a low wall with a seating plank built onto it at the top, called an ayimara. The clan houses had lands attached to them, and traditionally a designated senior male member of the clan lived there. He performed various duties at functions and festivals as also taking care of guests and visiting members of the clan. A clan member was entitled to have family functions like weddings held in the clan house.

Both the clan houses and private houses built around a century ago had provision for grain storage or pathaaya—either a room in the house or a structure outside.

A standard feature of the traditional houses was the hanging lamp in the entrance hall and a special prayer room, called the kannimoole kombaré. The hall was swept every morning and some water sprinkled on the floor. The hanging lamp was lit by the lady of the house in the morning and evening and prayers were said.

The special prayer room was an empty room bereft of images and religious symbols. There was a niche in a wall where an earthen lamp could be placed.

On special occasions and festivals a lamp was lit in the prayer room and offerings or meedi made to ancestors. When the meal for the occasion was cooked a small portion of each item was placed on a salver along with a glass of some alcoholic drink, taken to the prayer room and placed on the traditional three-legged stool—mukkali. When a married woman visited her natal home and wished to make offerings to her ancestors, she would bring with her food items including meat, which were cooked in the house and then offered. An earthen lamp was lit in the niche in the wall. The family gathered in the room and the oldest male handed small quantities of uncooked rice to each member and prayed aloud to the ancestors, asking for their protection and blessings. Each person would sprinkle some rice towards the lamp. The room was then closed and the offerings left inside. When the family sat down for the meal, the offerings were distributed amongst all the members. Meedi was not only offered to various ancestors but in one's own private home, to a dead parent or grandparent as well.

In some clan houses there was a separate pavilion type structure in front of the house which fulfilled the same function as the prayer room in the house. Here too, on special occasions offerings were made to ancestors.

Houses had earthen floors, stamped down, hardened and plastered over with cowdung. The floor plastering had to be renewed every so often. The roofs were always sloping to let the heavy rains run off, and were thatched with rice straw. In more recent times, the thatch has been replaced with roofing tiles and the cowdung for the flooring with cement or other materials. The walls of the old structures, however, remain and these were made of earth prepared in a special way. The bark and wood of a particular kind of tree that grows in the Kodagu jungles was chipped and put in a large container of water and allowed to ferment. Earth was mixed with this water and moulded into rounded lumps. A row of these was put up each day for the wall. When one row dried the next row was put on top. It is said that walls constructed in this way are as strong as granite. In any case, it is a fact that these old houses have stood for centuries without any sign of damage.

The old houses, whether clan or private, have a good deal of heavy wood-work, in this land of forests. Door frames are usually one foot thick or more. Sometimes one may see some carving on the wood-work as well. The doors do not have any hinges, but swivel in grooves in the frames at the top and bottom.

Kodagu houses sit easily on the landscape, blending beautifully with it. Usually they are built facing the valley, with the back of the house to the hill rising behind it. These houses, especially the clan houses, belong to an older architectural and social tradition, but there is no way of knowing how old they are. In more recent houses the traditional verandah and ayimara have been replaced by a porch. Contemporary houses, of course, do not necessarily conform to the traditional pattern.

The older temples in Kodagu resemble the temples of Kerala—one storey buildings with sloping tiled roofs, often with metal tiles and without domes or gopurams. The principal temple, the Talakavery is situated at the source of the holy river Kaveri. In addition to the temple there is a tiny shrine at the very spot where the river rises, gushing out in a spring, and in front of it is a tank where the devout can bathe. There are no such tanks in front of other temples, this one tank being a tribute to the holy river.

The Talakaveri temple and other temples are not architecturally notable, their importance being religious.

The temple at Talakaveri, attracts large numbers of pilgrims especially at the time of the Sankramana in October, marking the gushing out of the spring which becomes the river. This is called Theerthodbava (the rising of the sacred spring). The temple of Bhagamandala at the foot of the hill from where the Kavery rises is always an essential part of a visit to the Kavery. The other important temple sacred to the Kodava is dedicated to Igguthappa, the patron divinity of the local mountain.

*

Kodagu is rice country, so naturally in Kodava cuisine, rice is the basic item and plays a significant role in traditional food though now wheat, ragi, etc., are also used. In the past when jungles were denser and more extensive and farm merged with forest, forest produce both vegetarian and non-vegetarian had a significant place in Kodava cuisine. With conservation, wild fowl, wild pig, deer, etc., no longer figure on the menu. With the shrinking of jungles, a large number of wild fruit and edible and medicinal leaves as also yams are no longer in great evidence. Several delicious types of wild mushrooms have become increasingly rare. However, people still manage to get some bamboo shoots, wild leafy vegetables, wild mangoes and a berry which is boiled to produce the local variety of vinegar called kaachambuli.

In the villages, the Kodavas grow their own vegetables. It is usual to have a frame for beans, pumpkin or ash gourd in the vicinity of the kitchen, as also a shallow pit, manured with wood-ash, for bitter gourd. After the rice harvest, in the vacant fields, they plant cucumber, pumpkin, beans and a variety of gourds. Bollari (Mangalore cucumber) indigenous to Kodagu and used extensively in Kodava cuisine is cultivated as well. Bollari is orange in colour, and if allowed to mature fully, can be stored for months and is used during the long monsoon period. The beans are allowed to go to seed and the seeds are stored for use in the kitchen. Extended monsoon months in Kodagu make food storage and preservation necessary, as fresh green vegetables are scarce during the rains.

Food items usually stored for the rainy season include different kinds of salted, dried fish and, before the days of wild life conservation, dried game meat. These items, and jaggery, which, in the past was the main sweetener (now overtaken by sugar) are stored on a ladder-like slatted wooden frame called bedaké fixed horizontally over the cooking area, where the wood-fires and the smoke, keep them dry. Salt is put in an earthenware pot slung in a rope frame or udi from the bedaké.

In the old days most farm families had a small fortune in kitchen utensils of copper, brass and white bell-metal. Earthenware pots called chatti were also much in use, especially for cooking meat and fish dishes which had kaachambuli added to them, and often even for rice or vegetables. In fact, most of the daily cooking was done in these pots. New pots were seasoned by boiling rice in them to stop the porosity and in the initial stages, extra oil had to be used for tempering the earthenware and to allow absorption by the pot. Having been painstakingly tempered, they were greatly valued by the housewife. Salt and dried fish were stored in earthenware pots called kudiké.

Metal utensils were of different shapes and sizes, depending on their usage.

As there was no piped water in the old days, water was carried from wells in narrow-mouthed brass or copper pots called bindegés. The water was stored in kadaayas, which were wide-mouthed large copper pots, about two to three feet in diameter. It was taken out of the kadaaya with a baacheratay—a coconut shell attached to a handle, about one metre long. A chembu, which is a small copper container, was used for removing small quantities of water from large vessels.

There are a number of steamed dishes in Kodava cuisine and a special steamer called a chekala was used. It is a cylindrical copper container, with a tight fitting lid, about twenty inches wide and twenty inches high. Another container fits into this, a few inches below the top. Water is poured into the outer container and the food to be steamed is placed in the inner one. The base of the inner container has holes cut in decorative patterns of stars, crescent moons, etc. to allow steam to rise from below.

Ghee rice and palau were cooked in a special copper vessel called tappalé. It has a broad base and gradually tapers upwards so that there is a relatively narrow opening at the top. This helps in preserving the flavour of the dish.

Kapi tappalé, a smaller version of the tappalé was used to brew coffee. In coffee-producing Kodagu, anytime was coffee time and tea was rarely, if ever, drunk. The coffee was kept warm at all times over a small subsidiary chuhla or fire, adjacent to the main fire. It was connected to the main chuhla through a hole in the side and some of the flames would escape from the main chuhla and keep the coffee warm.

Wide cylindrical pans called ganji were used for various purposes, while a baaluruli, a small round-bottomed pan with a long handle was used for frying eggs, or any small quantity of food. The long handle was necessary, while using wood fires, to protect you from burning your hands.

Thaliya or plates of various sizes were used for sundry purposes and included the plates used for steaming, which have straight edges measuring about one to one-and-a-half inches high.

Apart from the regular tava or griddle, there was a special stone tava used for frying dosai called a dosai kallu and an earthenware tava used for making oduputtu called wodu.

Traditionally all cooking utensils had curved bottoms, so that the flames of the wood fire could curl around them. Only a small quantity of oil is required for tempering spices for curries, when using round-bottomed pans.

In recent times, stainless steel and aluminium vessels for deep frying, and frying pans for shallow frying have taken over from brass and copper. With the gradual spread of cooking over gas and the logistics of mass production, flat-bottomed pans have become as common as round-bottomed ones.

*

In Kodagu everyday meals are fairly simple. Breakfast begins with one main item, rice roti, dosai or a puttu with vegetarian or non-vegetarian accompaniments. Plain boiled rice is invariably served for both lunch and dinner with vegetables and a meat or fish dish, followed by fresh fruit. Traditionally, when rice was served for lunch or dinner, a teaspoon of melted ghee was poured over it for flavour.

On special occasions like weddings, naming ceremonies etc., or even when there are special guests, it is usual to have about four to five courses—a puttu served with meat or chicken curry, followed by palau or ghee rice served with pachchadi, then plain boiled rice with vegetables and curd; the penultimate item is a paayasa and the last, as usual, fresh fruit.

In Kodagu, seasons and festivals have special foods associated with them. Various items like bamboo shoots, wild mango, tender jack fruit, and different types of wild green leafy vegetables are prepared according to the seasons. There are other items, now becoming rare, like a particular type of wild creeper, the leaves of which were crushed and juice made into a jelly. Similarly, juice of a another medicinal leaf was used to cook a paayasa considered good for health. The juice could also be mixed with rice flour, cooked to a thick, pudding-like consistency, sweetened and eaten as a puttu. The medicinal quality of this leaf appears only in a particular season at which time the creeper has a special fragrance. A wild yam called puththari yam (after the harvest festival) is boiled and served with jaggery syrup, grated coconut, sesame seeds and ghee.

Quite apart from food that was available in different seasons, certain items were considered good for health.

Thus it was considered good to eat chicken during the wet and usually cold monsoon, as it has a 'warming' effect on the body; so also horse gram juice, cooked to a thick consistency, and colocasia leaves called kembu. Tender bamboo, also considered 'warming' in the wet weather is available at the beginning of the monsoon.

The monsoon is also the season when fresh water fish is available in the rice fields and small streams and rivers of Kodagu. These were caught by fixing a bamboo frame where the water from the terraced fields ran down to the lower fields, or in the small streams and rivers. Larger varieties of fish in the streams that would leap upstream over the water to spawn in the banks or rice fields would be cut in midflight with knives, at night, by the light of hurricane lanterns. Fish in ponds were occasionally shot with guns. But in recent years the use of chemical fertilizers and pesticides in rice fields and pollution in the streams is making the seasonal fresh water fish a distant memory.

*

Kodava festivals start with *Ugadi*, the first day of the Hindu calendar, bringing in the New Year. The day starts with eating a mouthful of crushed neem leaves with jaggery and coconut. Neem is medicinal and considered a panacea for many illnesses. Eating neem leaves at the beginning of the year is symbolic of keeping good health all through the year. Jaggery and coconut helps to make the bitter neem palatable. The three items together are also considered symbolic of the resolve to face both the sweet and bitter experiences throughout the year. Breakfast usually consists of dosai or thaliaputtu with chutney, followed by rice paayasa. Some people make New Year's Day vegetarian. For lunch they have ghee rice with vegetable kurma, one or two other vegetable dishes, and a pachchadi.

The festival of *Kailmoortha* or *Kailpoludu* falls on 3 September in Kodagu. The task of transplanting paddy over, it is one of the two main breaks in the farming year (the other one being puththari the harvest festival). It is primarily a men's festival.

Before lunch, the families line up their weapons, guns, the two ceremonial knives worn with the ceremonial costume and some of their lighter implements. They first offer puja in the house, and later in the cattleshed (where the plough and other implements are usually kept). After a festive lunch, the young men used to go into the forests for a shoot in the old days, but this custom is not observed any longer as hunting is prohibited. As a substitute, men shoot at coconuts hung between two trees.

On this festival, lunch often is a big meal with kadumbuttu and pork curry, and, if special guests are invited, pulau and pachchadi, plain boiled rice and vegetables, followed by paayasa.

On *Kaveri Sankramana*, which falls on 18 October, only vegetarian food is served in Kodava households. Essentially a women's festival, food includes pumpkin curry and thaliaputtu.

In people's homes, a symbolic image of goddess Kaveri is made with a clean-white or red cloth folded into a small triangle the apex pointing upwards. The triangle is propped up on bamboo sticks pushed into a cucumber to make an arch to hold the triangle. Black glass bangles, symbolic of a married woman whose husband is alive—muthaide are placed in front of this image. A few pieces of jewellery are used to decorate the image and a puja is performed.

Puththari or the harvest festival comes around the end of November or early December, on a full moon day. In the evening there is a puja in the house and after sunset men and women in their traditional ceremonial costumes go to the fields with a lighted earthenware oil lamp on a salver. They cut a few sheaves of paddy, praise the Lord with cries of 'poli poli Deva' and bring the sheaves into the house. A few stalks are tied to the front door and on the hanging prayer lamp in the central hall of the house. Some are tied to the door of the cowshed, some to the granary or pathaaya and some to the box or sanduka where cash and jewellery are kept. This is symbolic of the hope that prosperity will always reign in the family.

A large dinner on puththari is celebrated with pork curry and kadumbuttu. The following day, lunch is a huge affair with kadumbuttu, pork curry and pulau. In addition, there is also sweet potato or the seasonal puththari yam served with jaggery syrup, fresh grated coconut, ghee and powdered cardamom. Dessert on this festival includes thambuttu, a sweet made of ripe bananas, roasted parboiled rice flour and fenugreek powder, served with accompaniments of grated coconut, roasted sesame seeds, and ghee.

*

Generally speaking, Kodava food is light, like most South Indian food. Fat is only minimally used, mainly for tempering. Spices, too, are sparingly used, the aim being, as in much of South Indian cuisines, to enjoy the flavour of the item being cooked.

Traditional food was based on what was locally available, since commercially grown or distributed meat and vegetables were, on the whole, not readily available. Dry climate produce like pigeon peas and onions came in from the plains.

However the situation has changed inevitably over time. Items that were available from farm and forest of the past are no longer available, and items that were not available in the past are now available in the small rural towns, thanks to commercial production and distribution. Although the cuisine and food tastes are now influenced by other food traditions, a large body of traditional Kodava cuisine still persists.

The recipes in the book mention original ingredients. But alternatives can be used, both for ingredients as well as for utensils. Alternative ingredients, would of course, produce a difference in flavour.

Helpful Hints for Kodava Cuisine

Spices:

Traditionally all spices, including turmeric were freshly ground on the day of cooking. This produced a flavour that cannot compare with the flavour produced by today's packaged spice powders. A good compromise is to buy whole spices, clean well, grind and store in airtight containers. Grind just enough for one month's use as ground spices tend to lose flavour if kept too long.

Dry Roasting spices:
When dry roasting a number of different spices together, the spices that take the longest to roast are added to the pan first. The spices used, vary from recipe to recipe, but should be roasted in the order given below:

Black peppercorn
Cinnamon
Cloves
Coriander seeds
Fenugreek seeds
Cardamom seeds
Cumin seeds
Mustard seeds
Powdered spices

Heat a tava or griddle well. Reduce heat and add spices, one after the other stirring constantly. Roast each ingredient for a few seconds before adding the next. Take care that none of the ingredients burn.

Mustard seeds:
Mustard seeds used in Kodava cuisine are always the black variety (sarson).

Cardamom:
Only green cardamom is used in Kodava cuisine.

Tempering:
Tempering consists of frying whole spices in a little

fat—ghee or oil, traditionally coconut oil, and adding the main dish to the spices, towards the end of the cooking process.

The fat should be well heated before the spices are added. To test if it is ready flick in a drop of water with your.fingers. If the fat splutters it is ready. The spices used, depend on the dish to be prepared, but the order of adding them is important, so that the full flavour of each is brought out. The spices should be added to the fat in the following order:

Mustard seeds
Cumin seeds
Dried red chilli
Asafoetida (hing)
Garlic
Curry leaves
Onions

Mustard seeds must be allowed to splutter before the next ingredient is added. Each of the remaining ingredients should be allowed to fry for a few seconds before the next is added. Onions must always be put in last as otherwise the other ingredients will not fry well and their full flavour will not be brought out. Curry leaves may be added along with the onions.

In Kodava cuisine, fats are minimally used. This was easy in the old days when round-bottomed pans were used. Today you can use a kadahi or small pan. Heat fat and fry the spices. Add a little of the main dish to fried spices, stir and pour back into the main dish.

Cooking medium:
Ghee and vegetable oils are both used in Kodava cuisine, but where ghee is mentioned, try to use it, as oil will not give the same flavour.

Traditionally coconut oil and ghee were the medium of cooking.

Coconut:
Freshly grated and ground coconut, or the extracted milk is used in several dishes in Kodava cuisine. Only the white part of the coconut is used.

To make coconut milk:
Grate one fresh coconut (white part only). Add two cups hot water and allow to soak for 10 minutes. Squeeze with your hands and strain out water. This is the first or thick coconut milk. Add 2 cups more water to drained coconut and repeat the process. This gives the second or thin milk.

The thick milk, ground or grated fresh coconut must be added towards the end of the cooking process, to get the best flavour. The thin milk can be added to a dish at an earlier stage of cooking. The thin and thick milk can be mixed and added together towards the end of the cooking process.

Kaachambuli:
Kaachambuli is a special vinegar used in Kodava cuisine. It is made by boiling a local berry and is not normally available outside Kodagu. Substitutes like lime, malt vinegar or even ripe tomatoes can be used. These of course do not give the same flavour. Malt

vinegar is the best substitute. However kaachambuli is much stronger than vinegar and the quantity of vinegar used should be increased by half in the recipes mentioning kaachambuli.

Kaachumbuli is usually added to meat and fish dishes, while tamarind is used to flavour vegetable dishes.

When adding any sour item to a dish it is added just as the dish is being taken off the heat, as cooking sour items tends to make the dish bitter.

Jaggery:

Jaggery is the traditional sweetener in Kodava cuisine. However, sugar or brown sugar may be used in its stead.

To make jaggery syrup:

Add one cup hot water to jaggery the size of a lime. Allow to soak for 10 minutes. Stir to dissolve. Strain to remove grit and bits of sugarcane.

Adding salt or sugar to a dish:

When dal, beans or meat are being cooked, add the salt or sugar after they are tender. Adding salt or sugar earlier prevents from getting tender. This does not apply if a pressure cooker is used.

Adding green masala to a dish:

Green masalas containing green chillies, coriander leaves ginger, garlic and coconut are also added towards the end of the cooking process to preserve the flavour.

TABLE OF MEASURES

The cup measure used in this book is a 6 ounce Teacup.

1 tsp = 5 ml
1 tbsp = 3 tsp
A pinch = less than ⅛ tsp (literally a pinch)

Whenever teaspoons and tablespoons are mentioned in the book, use heaped measures unless stated otherwise.

30 gm = 1 oz
225 gm = 8 oz
450 gm = 1 lb
1 kg = 2.2 lb

170 ml = 6 oz
225 ml = 8 oz (American cup)
285 ml = 10 oz (Imperial cup)
450 ml = 16 oz (1 pint)

Rice

As in most parts of India, cereals are the centre of a meal—meat, fish or vegetables being accompaniments. In Kodagu the staple cereal is rice. It is cooked in a variety of ways, and eaten practically at every meal. We have therefore started the recipe section of the book with rice.

Boiled rice is eaten normally at lunch and dinner. It can be cooked either by adding just enough water to cook the rice, or with a large quantity of water which is drained out when the rice is cooked, but this diminishes the flavour and nutritional value.

Always use good quality rice while preparing rice dishes like ghee rice, palau and puttu. In Kodagu, the local rice sannakki is used. It is small grained, very soft when cooked, and has its own aroma. Sannakki is not readily available outside Kodagu, so basmati rice may be used.

Sannakki is preferred in Kodagu, just as basmati is preferred in North India.

Parboiled rice:
Kodava cuisine also makes use of parboiled rice. Unhusked rice is boiled, allowed to dry and then husked. It is readily available in most grocery shops across the country.

To cook plain boiled rice:
Wash rice and soak in double the quantity of water for 30 minutes. Place on heat, bring to boil, reduce heat and simmer for 20 minutes, till tender. Check if more water is required after about 15 minutes. Soaking the rice makes it cook more evenly.

AKKI OTTI

Rice Roti

Serves: 2-3

2 cups cooked rice
1½ cups rice flour
Salt to taste

- Mix rice, flour and salt in a bowl or thali. Add water, a little at a time and knead to make a dough of medium consistency.
- Pinch off a large lime-sized piece of dough and roll out into a roti 6-7 inches in diameter. Flatten edges with the heel of your palm.
- Heat a tava or griddle and cook for about 1-3 minutes on both sides.
- Put roti over direct flame for a few seconds to puff up. Do not allow roti to get brown spots.
- Make each roti in the same way.

Note: Akki otti is normally served at breakfast with a variety of chutneys and ghee or butter. It can also be served with curry.

The proportion of cooked rice and rice flour may be altered to taste. Increasing the quantity of the flour makes the roti crisper.

BENNÉ KADUBU

Steamed Rice Balls

Serves: 4-6

½ kg sannakki or basmati rice
1 cup grated fresh coconut
Salt to taste

- Wash rice and grind fine with coconut, adding water to make a batter of pouring consistency (like thin cream). Add salt and mix well.
- Put batter in a pan and boil stirring constantly till it reaches the consistency of a dough. Allow to cool.
- Rub palms with water or oil. Pinch off lime-sized pieces of dough. Form into balls and steam in a chekala or steamer. To test if done, pierce with a skewer. It should come out clean.
- Serve with chicken curry.

KADUMBUTTU

Steamed Rice Balls

Serves: 4-5

2 cups broken sannakki or basmati rice
Salt to taste

- Wash rice and place in a pan with 4 cups water and salt. Place pan on high heat and bring to boil. Lower heat and cook, stirring constantly till it reaches the consistency of a soft dough. Take care that dough does not stick to pan or burn. Remove pan from heat and let it continue cooking in its own heat for a further 10 minutes.
- Moisten palms with water or ghee and while dough is still hot, pinch off lime-sized pieces and shape into balls. Steam in a chekala or steamer till done. To test if done, pierce with a skewer. It should come out clean.
- Serve with pork curry.

Note: Kadumbuttus keep for several days and can be stored and re-steamed when required.

In the village kadumbuttus were cooked in large quantities before house guests arrived.

SANNA

Steamed Rice Cakes

Serves: 4-5

You will need idli moulds, metal katoris, ramekins or an egg poacher for this dish.

1 cup parboiled rice
1 cup rice
1 fresh coconut (grated)
Salt to taste
1 level tbsp dry yeast
1 tsp sugar dissolved in 3 tbsp warm water
1 tsp bicarbonate of soda

- Soak yeast in sugar syrup for half an hour.
- Wash both parboiled rice and ordinary rice and soak in water for about 3 hours.
- Drain rice, mix with grated coconut and grind to a very smooth paste. Add a little water while grinding, if necessary. The ground mixture should have the consistency of a thick pouring batter. Add salt and yeast.
- Leave overnight in a covered pan to ferment.
- Add bicarbonate of soda and stir mixture thoroughly until frothing.
- Grease an idli mould with oil or ghee, ladle mixture into moulds and steam for about 20 minutes or until

done. To test if done, pierce with a skewer. It should come out clean.

- Sannas are served for breakfast or as the first course of a festive dinner. They are usually eaten with chicken or pork curry.

MOR KOOLU

Curd Rice

Serves: 3-4

2 cups sannakki or basmati rice
Salt to taste
3 cups curd
1-2 green chillies (deseeded and finely chopped)
1 onion (finely chopped)
1 small bunch coriander leaves (finely chopped)
½ tsp grated ginger (optional)

For tempering:

2 tbsp oil
½ tsp mustard seeds
½ dried red chilli
5-6 curry leaves

- Wash rice and soak in 4 cups water for 30 minutes in a pan. Place pan on high heat and bring to boil. Lower heat and simmer till rice is tender, and water is absorbed. You may need to add a little more water during the process.
- While rice is still warm (not hot), add salt, curd, green chillies, onion, coriander leaves and ginger. Mix well.
- Heat oil for tempering in a small pan, add mustard seeds and allow to splutter. Add red chilli and then curry leaves. Fry for a few seconds.

- Add tempering to rice and curd mixture.
- Mix well. Serve with a dry meat or vegetable curry, or a pickle.

Note: Curd rice is not normally served as a regular dish. It is specially prepared to carry on journeys and is packed in a wilted banana leaf.

NEYI KOOLU

Ghee Rice

Serves: 3-4

2 cups sannakki or basmati rice
1 cup + 1 tbsp ghee
10 cloves
10 sticks cinnamon (1" each)
10 green cardamoms (whole)
10 large cloves garlic (crushed)
2 medium-sized onions (finely sliced)
¼ cup cashewnuts
¼ cup sultanas (kishmish)
Salt to taste

- Wash rice and soak in 4 cups water for half an hour before use.
- Heat one cup ghee in a pan (preferably with a curved bottom). Add cloves, cinnamon and cardamoms. Fry for a few seconds. Add garlic. When it begins to colour, add onions and fry till golden. Add cashewnuts and sultanas. Cook for a few seconds more.
- Drain rice, retaining water. Put rice into pan containing spices and continue frying for 1-2 minutes.
- Add reserved water, stir well, bring to boil on low heat and when rice is half cooked, stir in salt. Continue cooking till rice is tender.

- Pour over 1 tablespoon ghee, mix well and serve with a curry and pachchadi.

Variation: Instead of 4 cups water use 2 cups water and 2 cups coconut milk. Soak rice in 2 cups water. Add coconut milk when rice is half cooked.

NOOLPUTTU

String Hoppers

Serves: 3-4

Traditionally Noolputtu is pressed through a special noolputtu mould to produce noodle like strands of the steamed rice dough. A potato ricer or sevian machine may be used.

2 cups broken rice
Salt to taste

- Wash rice and place in a pan with 4 cups water and salt. Place pan on high heat and bring to boil. Lower heat and cook, stirring constantly till it reaches the consistency of a soft dough. Take care that dough does not stick to pan. Remove pan from heat and leave until dough is cool enough to handle, but still warm.
- Pinch off pieces of dough the size of an orange, shape into rounds and steam in a chekala or steamer till done. To test if done, pierce with a skewer. It should come out clean.
- Remove rice balls from chekala and while still hot, press through a noolputtu mould, sevian machine or potato ricer onto a plate.
- Serve with chicken curry.

ODUPUTTU

Rice Pancakes

Serves: 6-8

Oduputtu is traditionally cooked on an earthenware tava called Wodu. A regular tava, griddle or dosai pan (plain or nonstick) may be used. However, using earthenware gives a more authentic flavour and texture. The wodu was greased using a small piece of the midrib of a banana leaf dipped in castor oil.

1 kg rice
1 tbsp fenugreek seeds (methi)
1 cup cooked rice
Salt to taste
2 tbsp oil

- Wash rice and grind with remaining ingredients except oil. Add water during the process to get a fine batter of thick pouring consistency.
- Heat a Wodu, regular tava, griddle or dosai pan.
- Grease tava with a piece of cloth or a small piece of the midrib of a banana leaf dipped in oil. Pour one ladle of batter on tava. Swivel and roll tava to spread batter, cover and cook on low heat till done.
- Turn onto a plate and serve immediately with chutney and ghee or butter.
- Make remaining oduputtu in the same way, greasing tava each time.

Note: In this recipe the batter is not fermented.

PAAPUTTU

Steamed Rice Cakes with Coconut

Serves: 3-4

Normally thalis (flat stainless steel plates, with straight edges rising up about 1-1½ inches), are used for steaming paaputtu. They are traditionally steamed in a chekala, but a regular steamer can be used.

2 cups broken sannaki or basmati rice
2 cups water
1 cup milk or medium thick coconut milk
A pinch of salt
1 cup grated fresh coconut
Powdered seeds of 3-4 green cardamoms

- Wash rice and soak in water and milk with salt for 30 minutes.
- Spread rice and liquid evenly in thalis, sprinkle grated coconut and cardamom powder on top.
- Steam in a chekala or steamer for about 30 minutes or pressure cook without weight on lid for 10 minutes.
- To test if done, pierce with a skewer. It should come out clean.
- If more than one thali is used, they should be placed over each other and separated by skewers or bamboo sticks.

- Serve with chicken curry.

Note: The broken rice used to make paaputtu is slightly larger grained than semolina. If this is not available, grind regular broken rice coarsely before using.

Variation: **Modra Paaputtu (Steamed sweet rice cakes with Coconut)**

Dissolve one tbsp sugar in the water before soaking rice. Cook as given above.

Serve with ghee for breakfast or afternoon tea.

THALIAPUTTU

Steamed Rice Pancakes

Serves: 3-4

Flat stainless steel thalis or plates with 1½" high straight edges are required for this dish. The thalis are placed traditionally in a chekala for steaming, but a regular steamer may be used.

2 cups sannakki or basmati rice
½ cup husked black beans (urad dal)
½ tsp fenugreek seeds (methi)
1 cup cooked rice
1 cup coconut milk
Salt to taste
1 level tsp bicarbonate of soda

- Wash rice and black beans and soak with fenugreek seeds in water for about 3 hours.
- Drain and grind to a smooth paste. Add cooked rice and grind again to a smooth paste. Add a little water to help in grinding.
- Add coconut milk and salt. Whip mixture, and leave overnight in a covered container.
- Stir in bicarbonate of soda.
- Pour mixture into thalis and steam in a chekala or steamer till done. To test if done, pierce with a skewer. It should come out clean.

- Serve with chutney or meat or vegetable curry.

Variation: **Modra Thaliaputtu (Steamed sweet rice pancakes)**

Substitute coconut milk with one cup sugar syrup made from 1½ tbsp sugar, or jaggery syrup made from 2" cube jaggery.

Add powdered seeds of 3-4 cardamoms and ½ cup finely chopped fresh coconut before steaming.

Serve with ghee for breakfast or afternoon tea.

DOSAI

Rice Pancakes

Serves: 4-6

Dosai are traditionally cooked on a special stone tava called dosai kallu. A regular tava, griddle or dosai pan (plain or non stick), may be used. The tava is greased with a small piece of the midrib of a banana leaf dipped in castor oil. A piece of cloth dipped in oil may be used.

2 cups rice
½ cup husked black beans (urad dal)
½ tsp fenugreek seeds (methi)
1 cup cooked rice
Salt to taste
½ tsp bicarbonate of soda
2 tsp castor oil

- Wash rice and black beans. Soak with fenugreek seeds in water for 3 hours. Drain and grind fine. Add cooked rice and salt and continue grinding till very smooth. Add water if necessary during the process to make a batter of thick pouring consistency.
- Leave overnight in a covered pan. (Traditionally 2 teaspoons toddy was added to the batter to make it ferment.)
- Add bicarbonate of soda to batter and stir well.
- Heat a tava or griddle. Grease it with a piece of cloth or a small piece of the midrib of a banana leaf dipped

in castor oil. Pour in one ladle of batter. Spread gently using circular movements of the ladle. Cover tava and cook on one side only.

- Turn out onto a plate, and serve immediately with a chutney and ghee or butter, or butter and honey.
- Make each dosai in the some way, greasing tava each time before pouring batter.
- A good dosai should be crisp underneath, soft and fluffy on top and about a quarter inch thick.

NEERDOSAI

Rice Pancakes

Serves: 4-6

½ kg rice
Salt to taste
¼ tsp powdered green cardamom seeds (optional)
2 tsp castor oil

- Wash rice and soak in water with salt for 10 hours before use. Drain water, add cardamom and grind to a very fine paste. Add water a little at a time while grinding to get the consistency of a thick pouring batter.
- Heat tava and grease with a piece of cloth or a small piece of the midrib of a banana leaf dipped in oil. Pour one ladle of neerdosai batter on tava and roll and swivel tava to spread batter into a pancake. Cook, covered, on one side only, till base is crisp and brown, but top is still soft.
- Turn out onto a plate, and serve immediately with chicken curry.
- Prepare remaining neerdosai in the same way, greasing tava before cooking each one.

YERCHI PALAU-I

Rice Cooked with Meat

Serves: 4-6

2 cups sannakki or basmati rice
¾ kg mutton
1 tsp chilli powder
1 tsp turmeric powder
Salt to taste
1 cup curd
Juice of ½ a lime
1 tbsp ghee

Ground to a fine paste:

5 green chillies
2 onions
10 large cloves garlic
1" piece ginger
1 tsp cumin seeds
1½ tsp coriander powder
1 tsp poppy seeds (khus khus)
½ tsp black peppercorn
2 cloves
1" piece cinnamon
1 medium-sized bunch coriander leaves
½ fresh coconut (grated)

For tempering:

½ cup ghee
10 cloves
10 sticks cinnamon (1" each)

10 green cardamoms (whole)
10 cloves garlic (whole)
2 onions (chopped)
5-6 cashewnuts

- Wash rice and soak in 4 cups water for half an hour. Drain and keep aside, reserving water. Cut meat into one-and-a-half inch pieces, mix with chilli powder, turmeric and salt and leave to marinate for 20 minutes.
- Heat ½ cup ghee for tempering in a pan. Add cloves, cinnamon and cardamom and fry on low heat for a few seconds. Add garlic, and fry till it starts to colour. Add chopped onions and fry till golden. Add cashewnuts and stir for a few seconds more. Add ground masala and cook for 1-2 minutes.
- Add meat and curd, and cook on low heat till meat is nearly done, adding a little water if necessary. Put in soaked and drained rice and lime juice (it prevents the rice grains from sticking). Fry for 3-4 minutes.
- Heat reserved rice water in another pan and add to rice-meat mixture.
- Heat a tava and place pan on it. Cover pan and cook on low heat till rice is tender and water is absorbed.
- Before taking pan off the heat, sprinkle one tablespoon ghee on top.

Note: Instead of 4 cups water, 3 cups water and 1 cup coconut milk can be used. Soak rice in 3 cups water and add coconut milk when rice is half cooked.

Variation: **Yerchi Palau - II**
Follow the recipe above, but cook meat with chilli powder, turmeric, salt and curd till tender, adding a little water if necessary. Dry out excess water and add to fried spices. Continue as given.

Koli Palau (Rice cooked with chicken)
Use chicken in place of mutton in either recipe.

Meat and Poultry

YERCHI BARTA KARI-I

Dry Mutton Masala

Serves: 6-8

1 kg mutton (cut into 1½" pieces)
½ tsp turmeric powder
½ tsp chilli powder
½ cup oil
Salt to taste
1 tsp kaachambuli or 1½ tsp malt vinegar

Ground to a fine paste with a little water:
5 medium-sized onions
10 cloves garlic
½" piece ginger
4 cloves
2 tsp poppy seeds (khus khus)
4 sticks cinnamon (1" each)
2-3 green chillies (deseeded)
2 tsp black peppercorn

- Mix mutton with turmeric and chilli powder and leave to marinate for half an hour.
- Heat oil in a pan, add ground masala and fry on low heat for 2-3 minutes till oil separates and masala turns dark brown.
- Add mutton and fry, stirring for 10 minutes. Add 2 cups water, stir and cover pan. Cook on low heat till mutton is half done. Add salt, stir and cook till mutton is tender.

- Add kaachambuli, stir and remove from heat.
- The mutton, when cooked should have absorbed most of the water and have only a little gravy left.
- Serve with akki otti or boiled rice.

Variation: **Koli Barta Kari - I (Dry Chicken Masala)**
Substitute chicken in place of mutton.

YERCHI BARTA KARI-II

Dry Mutton Masala

Serves: 6-8

1 kg mutton (cut into 1½" pieces)
1 tsp turmeric powder
½ tsp chilli powder
½ cup oil
2 cloves garlic (crushed)
2 onions (chopped)
½" piece ginger (finely chopped)
Salt to taste
½ tsp kaachambuli or ¾ tsp malt vinegar

Masala for grinding:

1 tsp black peppercorn
4 sticks cinnamon (1" each)
6 cloves
A pinch of fenugreek seeds (methi)
1 tbsp coriander powder
1 tsp cumin seeds
A pinch of mustard seeds
Seeds of 1 green cardamom

- Mix mutton with turmeric and chilli powder and leave aside to marinate for 30 minutes.
- Heat a tava or griddle and add ingredients for masala to be ground to tava in the order given, and dry roast. Roast each ingredient for a few seconds before adding next. Grind fine.

- Heat oil in a pan and add crushed garlic. The moment it turns colour, add onions and ginger. Fry on low heat till onions begin to brown. Add ground spices and cook on low heat for 2-3 minutes. Add mutton, stir and cook for 2 minutes. Add 1-2 cups water and cook till mutton is tender—about 1-1½ hours. Add salt to taste.
- When cooked, the curry should be semi-dry. Add kaachambuli, stir and remove immediately from heat.

Variation: **Koli Barta Kari - II (Dry Chicken Masala)**
Substitute chicken in place of mutton.

YERCHI KANNI KARI

Mutton Curry

Serves: 4-6

1 kg mutton (cut into 1½" pieces)
1 tsp turmeric powder
2 tsp coriander powder
3 tbsp oil
1 onion (chopped)
Salt to taste
1 tsp kaachambuli or 1½ tsp malt vinegar

Ground to a fine paste:

2 onions
10 cloves garlic
6 cloves
4 sticks cinnamon (1" each)
1 green cardamom (peeled)
1 tsp cumin seeds
1 tsp poppy seeds (khus khus)
4 cups water

Ground to a fine paste:

½ fresh coconut (grated)
2 green chillies
1 bunch coriander leaves

- Mix mutton with turmeric and coriander powder and marinate for 10 minutes.
- Heat oil in a pan, add chopped onions and fry till

light brown.

- Add ground onion masala and fry on low heat for 2 minutes. Add mutton and continue frying on low heat for about 10 minutes. Add water and increase heat to quickly bring to boil. Lower heat and simmer till mutton is tender. There should be enough water to cook the mutton and have a good quantity of gravy.
- Add ground coconut masala and salt and stir for 1-2 minutes.
- Add kaachambuli or vinegar, stir and remove immediately from heat.

Variation: **Koli Kanni Kari (Chicken Curry)**
Substitute chicken for mutton.

PANDI KARI

Pork Curry

Serves: 4-6

1 kg pork (including fatty pieces) cut into 1½" pieces
1 tsp turmeric powder
1 tsp chilli powder
1" piece ginger
5 cloves garlic
1 onion
Salt to taste
2 tsp kaachambuli or 3 tsp malt vinegar

Dry masala for grinding:

1 tsp black peppercorn
5 sticks cinnamon (1" each)
6 cloves
1 tsp cumin seeds
2 tsp coriander powder

Ground to a fine paste:

1 cup chopped onions
1" piece ginger
5 cloves garlic
5 green chillies (deseeded)
1 tsp cumin seeds

- Mix pork with turmeric powder and chilli powder. Leave to marinate for 15 minutes.
- Heat a tava or griddle reduce heat and add

ingredients for dry masala to be ground in the order given. Roast each ingredient for a few seconds before adding next. Grind to a fine paste with ginger, garlic and onion. Add to pork and mix well.

- Boil 3 cups water, and add pork and ground onion masala. Stir, cover and cook till pork is half done. Add salt. Stir well, cover and cook till pork is tender and gravy is thick.
- Add kaachambuli or vinegar, stir and remove immediately from heat.
- Serve with kadumbuttu, akki otti or plain boiled rice.

Note: Usually spices are not fried for tempering when cooking pork curry, because of the fat in the meat. But if the pork is very lean, one or two tablespoons of oil should be added to the curry when the pork is added to the water. Pork curry can be stored for several days and reheated.

Traditionally, the fatty pieces of pork are cooked with the skin attached. When the skin is tender, the curry is ready.

CHIDUKUWA

Preserved Pork

This is a traditional method of preserving pork in its own fat, without drying or salting. It belongs to the times when the only way to have pork in the villages was to kill a pig on the farm, since markets and shops were not easily accessible and in any case pork was not sold.

Since a large quantity of pork could not be used up quickly, it had to be preserved. A special pan about twenty inches wide with a curved bottom, called a chidukuwa pan was used. It was very shallow, about eight inches deep, made of copper and tinned on the inside.

Pork
¼ tsp turmeric powder per kg of pork
½ tsp salt per kg of pork

- Cut pork into 2" pieces. Arrange pork pieces into 3 groups—fat, fat and lean and lean. Place pan on heat, add 6 cups water and turmeric powder and bring to boil.
- Add fatty pork pieces and cook till fat melts and water evaporates. Add fat-and-lean pieces. Cook till fat begins to ooze out. Add lean pieces of pork. Stir occasionally and when half cooked add salt.
- Cover and cook till pork is tender. Remove from heat and cool.

- To store, place in a clean, dry ganji or large jars and ensure that fat covers the meat completely. Cover and store.

Note: This is delicious eaten as it is after heating or it can be taken out in small quantities to make pork curry.

Fish and Prawns

In Kodagu, fish is usually first washed in water that has a little kaachambuli mixed in it. This removes the fishy smell and sliminess. Alternatively vinegar, lime-juice or salt can be added to the water.

Large fleshy varieties of fish like surmai or bekti are cut into pieces (about 1½" cubes) or sliced through the bone. Smaller varieties of fish like mackerel or sardines are usually fried. The mackerel has to be slit on both sides before marinating with masala.

BARTA MEEN

Fried Fish

Serves: 4-6

1 kg fish
1 tsp kaachambuli or 1½ tsp malt vinegar
1 tsp turmeric powder
2 tsp chilli powder
½ tsp black pepper powder
1 tsp ginger-garlic paste (optional)
Salt to taste
Oil for shallow frying

- Clean and wash fish in water mixed with a little extra kaachambuli. If a small variety of fish is being used, leave whole, otherwise cut into ¾" thick slices.
- Mix spices and salt with kaachambuli and a little water to make a paste. Roll pieces of fish individually in spices to cover thoroughly and marinate for 30 minutes.
- Put oil in a frying pan, and heat. Fry fish on low heat without covering pan turning pieces once only.

CHAṬṬÉ MEEN KARI

Prawn Curry

Serves: 2-3

½ kg shelled prawns (deveined and cleaned)
1 tsp turmeric powder
½ tsp chilli powder
1 tsp coriander powder
Salt to taste
2 tbs oil
½ tsp mustard seeds
2 cloves garlic (crushed)
1 onion (chopped)
½" piece ginger (finely chopped)
1 tsp kaachambuli or 2 tsp malt vinegar

Ground to a fine paste:
2 green chillies
2 onions

- Mix prawns with turmeric powder, chilli powder, coriander powder and salt.
- Leave aside to marinate for 20 minutes.
- Heat oil in pan, add mustard seeds and allow to splutter. Put in crushed cloves of garlic. As they begin to turn colour, add chopped onion, and ginger. Fry till onion turns golden.
- Add prawns and ground masala. Stir and fry lightly.
- Add one cup water and stir.

- Cook on low heat to reduce gravy.
- Just before removing from heat, add kaachambuli and stir.

MEEN KARI

Fish Curry

Serves: 4-6

1 kg fish
2 tbsp oil
½ tsp cumin seeds
2-3 cloves garlic (crushed)
1 onion (chopped)
5-6 curry leaves
1 tsp turmeric powder
½ tsp chilli powder
1 tsp coriander powder
Salt to taste
1½ tsp kaachambuli or 2¼ tsp malt vinegar

Ground to a fine paste:

½ fresh coconut (grated)
4-5 cloves garlic
1 onion
½" piece ginger
1-2 green chillies
1 bunch coriander leaves (optional)

- Clean and wash fish with water mixed with a little extra kaachambuli. Slice into 1" thick pieces.
- Heat oil in a pan, add cumin seeds and allow to splutter. Add crushed garlic and when it begins to colour, add chopped onions and curry leaves. Fry till onion turns golden brown. Add turmeric powder,

chilli powder, coriander powder and salt. Cook for a few minutes on low heat until spices are done. Fish cooks quickly and the masala, especially turmeric and chilli powder should not be undercooked by the time the fish is done.

- Add ground masala and 1½ cups water, to make a gravy. Simmer for 2-3 minutes.
- Add fish and stir gently so that fish pieces are coated with masala. Cook on low heat, shaking pan gently from time to time to prevent contents sticking to pan and taking care not to break the fish pieces.
- When fish is done, add kaachambuli and gently shake pan to roll the liquid around (to prevent fish from breaking). Remove from heat.
- Serve with boiled rice or akki otti.

Variation: **Koyilé Meen Kari (Paddy-field Fish Curry)**
Paddy-field fish is a variety of very small fish which is available in season in the paddy fields. After the paddy seedlings are transplanted, water is let into the fields, and this fish is available here. Thanks to the modern custom of using chemical fertilizers and pesticides, these fish are becoming a rarity.

The fish, when available, is cooked in the same way as fish curry and is served with akki otti or boiled rice.

ONNAK MEEN

Dried Salted Fish

Serves: 2

¼ kg dried fish
½ tsp turmeric powder
½ tsp chilli powder
2 tsp kaachambuli or 3 tsp malt vinegar
2 tbsp oil
3 onions (chopped into 1" pieces)
4 green chillies (slit lengthwise and deseeded)

- Cut fish into pieces, discarding bones. Soak in hot water for 15 minutes to desalt. Discard water. Repeat twice. Remove water completely, by gently squeezing fish.
- Marinate fish with turmeric powder, chilli powder and kaachambuli for 15 minutes.
- Heat oil in a pan, add onions and green chillies and stir till onions turn golden.
- Add fish and cook on low heat until tender. It should take about 10 minutes.

Vegetables

BAIMALÉ KARI

Tender Bamboo Shoot Curry

Serves: 6-8

Tender bamboo is available in Kodagu at the beginning of the monsoon. It is cut into thin slices about one inch wide and two inches long. It is put in a pan (traditionally earthenware) covered with water and left for 24 hours. It is drained out completely as one-day old bamboo water is toxic, rinsed in fresh water, and left to soak in enough water to cover for a further 48 hours. The bamboo and water ferment a little, turn slightly sour and are ready for use.

1 kg bamboo shoot pieces with water, treated as above
1 tsp turmeric powder
1 tsp chilli powder
Salt to taste

Dry masala for grinding:

1 tbsp rice
1 tsp cumin seeds
½ tsp mustard seeds

Ground to a fine paste:

¼ fresh coconut
1 onion
1 tsp coriander powder

For tempering:

2 tbsp oil
½ tsp mustard seeds
2 pieces dried red chilli (1" each, deseeded)
3-4 cloves garlic (crushed)
4-5 curry leaves

- Heat a tava or griddle and roast ingredients for dry masala to be ground in the order given. Roast each ingredient for a few seconds before adding next. Grind fine.
- Place bamboo shoot with water in which it was soaked for 48 hours, turmeric, chilli powder and salt in a pan, preferably earthenware. Cook till tender. It should take 30-40 minutes.
- Skim foam, if any. Reduce heat and add dry ground spices. Mix well.
- In a separate pan, heat oil for tempering put in mustard seeds and allow to splutter. Add red chillies, stir briefly, and add crushed garlic. When garlic begins to change colour, add curry leaves and ground masala paste. Stir and continue to fry for 2 minutes.
- Add tender bamboo shoot and cook for 2-3 minutes. There should only be a small quantity of gravy in this preparation.
- Serve with boiled rice or akki otti.

BOLLARI BARTHAD

Dry Mangalore Cucumber Curry

Serves: 4-6

1 kg Mangalore cucumber (bollari)
1 tsp turmeric powder
¾ tsp chilli powder
1 tsp coriander powder
Salt to taste
1" piece jaggery dissolved in 1 cup water

For tempering:

2 tbsp oil
¼ tsp mustard seeds
3-4 curry leaves
2 onions (chopped)

Ground to a fine paste:

¼ fresh coconut (grated)
¼ tsp cumin seeds
2 cloves garlic

- Cut open Mangalore cucumber and scoop out seeds. Discard. Cut flesh into one by three inch pieces without peeling. Add turmeric powder, chilli powder, coriander powder, salt and set aside for 30 minutes.
- Heat oil for tempering in a pan, add mustard seeds and fry till they start to splutter. Add chopped onion and curry leaves. Fry till onions begin to turn golden.

- Add cucumber and stir for one minute. Strain in jaggery syrup. Stir and cook on low heat for 10 minutes.
- When tender, add ground masala, stir and remove from heat.

Variation: **Nuggekai Barthad (Dry Drumstick Curry)**
Drumsticks may be used instead of Mangalore cucumber. In place of jaggery, use 1" square piece of tamarind soaked in one cup water. Add tamarind with ground masala, just before removing from heat.

BOODI KUMBALA MOR KANNI

Ash Gourd with Curd

Serves: 2-3

½ kg ash gourd (petha)
3 green chillies (deseeded and chopped)
Salt to taste
½ cup curd

Ground to a fine paste:

½ fresh coconut (grated)
¼ tsp mustard seeds
¼ tsp cumin seeds

For tempering:

2 tbsp oil
1 tsp mustard seeds
2 dried red chillies (deseeded and broken into 1" pieces)
3 cloves garlic (crushed)
4-5 curry leaves

- Peel and cut ash gourd into 1½" cubes. Boil with green chillies and salt in 2 cups water.
- When tender, add ground masala, mix well and keep aside.
- Heat oil for tempering in a pan, add mustard seeds and allow to splutter. Add red chillies and stir. Add crushed garlic and curry leaves. When garlic begins to turn golden, add ash gourd. Stir for 2 minutes.

- Add curd, and stir well. Remove immediately from heat.

Variation: **Kari Baalé Mor Kanni (Curry Bananas with Curd)**

Curry bananas can be cooked in the same way.

CHEKKÉ KARI

Raw Jack Fruit Curry

Serves: 4-6

1 kg peeled raw jack fruit (kathal)
1 cup pigeon peas (toover or arhar dal)
1 tsp coriander powder
1 tsp chilli powder
1 tsp cumin powder
½ fresh coconut (grated and ground to a paste)
Salt to taste
1 tsp tamarind juice

For tempering:

2 tbsp oil
1 tsp mustard seeds
2 dried red chillies (deseeded)
1 onion (chopped)
3-4 curry leaves

- Cut jack fruit into 1½" cubes.
- Wash pigeon peas and place in a pan with jack fruit and enough water to cover. Place pan on heat, cover and boil till dal and jack fruit are nearly cooked.
- Add coriander powder, chilli powder and cumin powder. Cook till jack fruit and dal are tender. Add ground coconut and salt, stir and set aside.
- In a separate pan, heat oil for tempering, put in mustard seeds and allow to splutter. Add red

chillies, stir for a few seconds and add onion and curry leaves. Fry till onion turns golden brown.

- Add jack fruit mixture and stir. Add tamarind juice, stir and remove from heat.

Variation: Raw jack fruit curry can also be cooked with black-eyed beans (lobia) soaked over-night.

KAI KUMBALA KARI

White Pumpkin Curry

Serves: 4-6

Use pumpkin with green skin for this recipe.

1 kg white pumpkin (kaddu)
1 level tsp turmeric powder
1 tsp coriander powder
Salt to taste

Ground to a fine paste:

¼ fresh coconut (grated)
2 green chillies (slit)
1" piece jaggery (optional)

For tempering:

2 tbsp oil
¼ tsp mustard seeds
1 dried red chilli (broken into pieces)
4 cloves garlic (crushed)

- Cut pumpkin into one inch cubes, including skin. Discard seeds. Place pumpkin in a pan with just enough water to cover, turmeric powder, coriander powder and salt. Cook on low heat till pumpkin is tender. Take care that the pumpkin does not cook to a pulp. There should be only a little gravy left in the pan.
- Add ground masala, stir and set aside.

- In a separate pan, heat oil for tempering, put in mustard seeds and allow to splutter. Add red chilli, stir briefly and add crushed cloves of garlic. When garlic begins to change colour, add pumpkin, stir and remove from heat.
- Serve with akki otti.

KAIPEKKÉ KARI

Dry Bitter Gourd Curry

Serves: 2

¼ kg bitter gourd (karela)
1 tbsp flour (maida)
1 tsp salt
2 tbsp oil
¼ tsp mustard seeds
4 cloves garlic (crushed)
4 medium-sized onions (chopped)
1 green chilli
3-4 curry leaves
½ tsp chilli powder
¼ tsp turmeric powder
1½ tsp coriander powder
3" piece jaggery dissolved in 1 cup water
Salt to taste

- Wash bitter gourd and slit vertically. Remove seeds.
- Rub with flour and one teaspoon salt and set aside for one hour. This removes the bitterness from the gourd. Wash bitter gourd and drain well.
- Heat oil in a pan, add mustard seeds and allow to splutter. Add crushed garlic. When garlic begins to change colour, add onions, green chilli and curry leaves. Fry till onion turns golden. Add chilli powder, turmeric and coriander. Fry till mixture is light brown.

- Add bitter gourd, strained jaggery syrup and salt to taste. Cook on low heat, till bitter gourd is tender and a small quantity of gravy is left.

KEMBU KARI

Colocasia Leaf Curry

Serves: 4-5

Always use tender colocasia leaves, as the mature ones cause itching in the mouth and tend to be coarse.

1 kg colocasia leaves (arvi patta)
1 cup pigeon peas (toover or arhar dal)
½ tsp turmeric powder
½ tsp chilli powder
1 tsp coriander powder
Salt to taste
½ fresh coconut (ground)
Juice of 1½ a lime

For tempering:

1 tbsp oil
¼ tsp mustard seeds
1-2 dried red chillies (deseeded)
3-4 cloves garlic (crushed)
3-4 curry leaves

- Wash and clean colocasia leaves. Remove central rib and cut into fine strips. Wash dal.
- Place dal and colocasia leaves in a pan with enough water to cover. Place pan on heat and bring to boil. Lower heat and simmer till tender.
- Add turmeric, chilli powder, coriander powder and salt. Stir and cook for 1-2 minutes further. Remove from heat.

- Heat oil for tempering in another pan, add mustard seeds and allow to splutter. Add red chillies. Stir and add garlic and curry leaves.
- When garlic begins to change colour, add colocasia leaves and pigeon peas with grated coconut. Cook for 2 minutes.
- Add lime juice and serve.

Note: Lime juice not only enhances the taste but also prevents itching in the mouth.

Variation: Instead of pigeon peas, colocasia leaves can also be cooked with black-eyed beans (lobiya) soaked overnight.

KOOTU KARI

Mixed Vegetable Curry

Serves: 2-3

In Kodagu French beans are allowed to run to seed. The seeds are then removed and dried.

½ kg mixed vegetables such as beans, knol khol (ganth gobi), potatoes, carrots
1-2 tomatoes (chopped)
¾ cup dried seeds of French beans, washed and soaked overnight
1 tsp coriander powder
1 tsp chilli powder
½ tsp cumin powder
¼ tsp turmeric powder
Salt to taste
½ fresh coconut (grated and ground to a paste)

For tempering:

2 tbsp oil
¼ tsp mustard seeds
1 onion (chopped)
3-4 curry leaves

- Boil beans till tender.
- Wash and cut vegetables into one inch cubes, add to boiled beans with tomatoes and 2 cups water. Place pan on heat and cook till vegetables are nearly done. Ensure mixture retains at least one cup water.
- Add coriander powder, chilli powder, cumin

powder, turmeric and salt. Stir and cook till vegetables are tender.

- Add coconut, stir and remove from heat.
- Heat oil for tempering in another pan. Add mustard seeds and allow to splutter. Add onion and curry leaves. Fry till onion is golden brown. Add vegetables and dal and cook for 2 minutes.
- Serve with neye koolu or boiled rice.

Note: Kootu is usually served when an entirely vegetarian meal is cooked on special occasions like Kaveri Sankramana.

KUMMU KARI

Mushroom Curry

Serves: 6-8

There are three main varieties of mushroom in Kodagu, all of which grow wild. Two of them are large—koday kummu (or umbrella mushrooms) and aalandi kummu—and one small variety, nuchi kummu. They grow in forests or rice fields after the monsoon and harvest. Mushrooms are picked early in the morning and cleaned, as they wilt soon after the sun comes up.

1 kg mushrooms
1 tsp chilli powder
½ tsp turmeric powder
2 tsp coriander powder
Salt to taste
2 tsp kaachambuli or 3 tsp malt vinegar

For tempering:

2 tbsp oil
¼ tsp mustard seeds
3 medium-sized onions (chopped)

Ground to a fine paste:

½ fresh coconut
1 tsp cumin seeds
4 cloves garlic

- Wash and clean mushrooms. Rub chilli powder,

turmeric powder, coriander powder and salt into mushrooms and set aside for 30 minutes.

- Put oil for tempering in a pan and heat. Put in mustard seeds and allow to splutter. Add chopped onions. Fry on low heat till onions are golden brown.
- Add mushrooms, stir and add 3 cups water. Cook on low heat till mushrooms are tender.
- Add ground masala and stir briefly. Add kaachambuli, stir and remove from fire.
- Serve with rice or akki otti.

MOLAI MUDARÉ KANNI

Sprouted Horse Gram with Vegetables

Serves: 3-4

1 cup sprouted horse gram (kulthi ka dal)
250 gms any of the following vegetables—aubergine (baigan), curry bananas, banana trunk, white radish, Mangalore cucumber (bollari) or bottle gourd (ghia)
1 tsp coriander powder
¼ tsp turmeric powder
½ tsp chilli powder
Salt to taste
¼ fresh coconut (ground)

For tempering:

2 tbsp oil
¼ tsp mustard seeds
4 cloves garlic (crushed)
4-5 curry leaves
1 onion (chopped)

- Wash horse gram and boil in 2-3 cups water till tender.
- Wash and cut chosen vegetable into 1" cubes.
- Add vegetables to horse gram with coriander, turmeric and chilli powder and cook on low heat till vegetables are tender. Add coconut paste and salt and stir. Set aside.
- Heat oil for tempering in another pan, add mustard

seeds and allow to splutter. Add garlic and fry till it colours. Add curry leaves and onion and fry till onions turn golden brown. Pour in cooked vegetables and horse gram, stir and remove from heat.

- Serve with rice.

Note: In this preparation, there should be a fair amount of gravy.

MUDARÉ KANNI

Horse Gram Gravy

Makes: 1 cup

In the days when horsegram was boiled in large quantities for bullocks on the farm, the horse gram was fed to the bullocks and the water in which it was boiled was made into this very traditional 'gravy', which was eaten with boiled rice or akki otti.

1 kg horsegram (kulthi ka dal)
Tamarind the size of a large lime
2" piece jaggery
1 tsp coriander powder
½ tsp turmeric powder
½ tsp chilli powder
Salt to taste
5 tbsp oil
½ tsp mustard seeds

Ground to a fine paste:

1 onion
10 cloves garlic

Dry masala for grinding:

2 tbsp black peppercorn
½ tsp fenugreek seeds (methi)
4 pieces dried red chilli (1" each)
2 tsp cumin seeds

- Wash horsegram and boil with one litre water for 1½ hours, or pressure cook for 45 minutes. Strain and reserve water. Use gram for any other purpose.
- Soak tamarind and jaggery in one cup horse gram water. Squeeze and strain liquid.
- Mix coriander, turmeric, chilli powder and salt into remaining horsegram water.
- Heat a tava or griddle and add 2 teaspoons oil. Add ingredients for dry masala to be ground, one at a time in the order given, stirring continuously to prevent burning. Allow each ingredient to fry for a few seconds before adding next. Grind fine. Mix with onion and garlic paste.
- Heat remaining oil in a pan. Add mustard seeds and allow to splutter. Add ground masala and fry on low heat for 2 minutes, stirring constantly to prevent masala from sticking or burning.
- Add horsegram water and tamarind and jaggery water. Mix and cook till gravy is reduced, stirring frequently to avoid burning. When ready it should have the consistency of thin custard.
- Serve with boiled rice or akki otti.

Note: Mudaré kanni can be preserved for several days. To help thicken the gravy grind one cup boiled gram, fine and mix into horsegram water. Alternatively, add a paste of one tsp rice flour and 2 tbsp water and cook to thicken.

KURU KARI

French Bean Seed Curry

Serves: 3-4

This curry is traditionally made with the French beans grown in Kodagu, which are allowed to run to seed. The seeds are black in colour. You may use red kidney beans (rajma), but the texture and flavour will be different.

½ kg French bean seeds (soaked overnight)
½ tsp turmeric powder
1 tsp chilli powder
2 tsp coriander powder
Salt to taste

For tempering:

2 tbsp oil
¼ tsp mustard seeds
2 dried red chillies (deseeded)
10 cloves garlic (crushed)
1 onion (chopped)
3-4 curry leaves

Ground to a fine paste:

½ fresh coconut
½ tsp cumin seeds
4 cloves garlic
1" piece tamarind without seeds or fibre (or one tsp tamarind juice)
1 small bunch coriander leaves

- Boil bean seeds with enough water to cover, turmeric, chilli and coriander powder till tender. Add salt.
- Heat oil for tempering in another pan and add mustard seeds. Allow to splutter. Add red chillies, stir for a few seconds, and add crushed garlic. When garlic begins to turn golden, add chopped onions and curry leaves. Fry till onions are golden brown.
- Add beans and allow to cook for a few minutes.
- Add ground masala and stir. Cook for a minute and remove from heat.
- Serve with boiled rice or akki otti.

TARKARI KANNI KARI - I

Vegetable Curry with Lentils

Serves: 4-6

Vegetable curry cooked with pigeon peas is a regular item on the daily menu. Traditional local vegetables are used, but you may substitute them with any of your choice.

½ kg any of the following vegetables—aubergines (baigan), Mangalore cucumber (bollari), French beans, curry bananas, bottle gourd (ghia), ridge gourd (toori) or snake gourd (chirchinda)
¾ cup pigeon peas (toover or arhar dal)
½ tsp turmeric powder
½ tsp chilli powder
1 tsp cumin powder
1½ tsp coriander powder
Salt to taste
¼ fresh coconut (grated and ground to a paste)
1 tsp tarmarind paste

For tempering:

2 tbsp oil
¼ tsp mustard seeds
1" piece dried red chilli (deseeded)
3-4 curry leaves
1 onion (chopped)

- Wash and chop chosen vegetable into 1" pieces.
- Wash pigeon peas and boil with 3 cups water till soft.

- Add vegetable with turmeric, chilli powder, cumin powder, coriander powder and salt. Cook till done. Add ground coconut and tamarind paste. Stir and remove from heat.
- Heat oil for tempering in another pan, add mustard seeds and allow to splutter. Add red chilli, then curry leaves and chopped onion. When onion begins to turn golden brown, add cooked dal and vegetable, stir and remove from heat.
- Serve with boiled rice.

Note: The dal cooks faster if it is soaked in advance for about 30 minutes.

TARKARI KANNI KARI-II

Vegetable Curry with Lentils

Serves: 6

½ kg any of the following vegetables—aubergines (baigan), Mangalore cucumber (bollari), French beans, curry bananas, bottle gourd (ghia), ridge gourd (toori) or snake gourd (chirchinda)

¾ cup pigeon peas (toover or arhar dal)

½ tsp turmeric powder

2½ tsp coriander powder

Salt to taste

Grind to a fine paste:

¼ fresh coconut (grated)

1 tsp tamarind paste

1 tsp cumin powder

2 cloves garlic

1 green chilli (deseeded)

For tempering:

2 tbsp oil

¼ tsp mustard seeds

1" piece dried red chilli (optional)

1 onion (chopped)

3-4 curry leaves (optional)

- Wash and chop chosen vegetable into 1" pieces.
- Wash dal and boil in 3 cups water till soft.
- Add vegetable, turmeric powder, coriander powder

and salt. Cook till tender.

- Add ground masala. Stir and remove from heat.
- Heat oil for tempering in another pan, add mustard seeds. Allow to splutter, add red chilli and fry for a few seconds. Add onion and curry leaves and fry till onion turns golden brown. Pour in cooked vegetable mixture and stir well.
- Serve with boiled rice.

TOGAY

Pigeon Peas

Serves: 2-3

1 cup pigeon peas (toover or arhar dal)
3 medium-sized onions (chopped)
2 green chillies (chopped)
3 ripe tomatoes (chopped)
¼ tsp turmeric powder
¼ tsp chilli powder
½ tsp coriander powder
Salt to taste
1" piece jaggery dissolved in ¼ cup water

For tempering:

1 tbsp oil
¼ tsp mustard seeds
1 dried red chilli
4 cloves garlic (crushed)
5-6 curry leaves

Ground to a fine paste:

¼ fresh coconut (grated)
¼ tsp cumin seeds
2 cloves garlic

- Wash dal and boil with onions, chillies and tomatoes in 3 cups water till tender.
- Add turmeric powder, chilli powder, coriander powder, salt and strained jaggery syrup. Stir and

cook for 2-3 minutes.

- Heat oil for tempering in another pan, add mustard seeds and allow to splutter. Add red chilli, fry for a few seconds and add crushed garlic. When garlic turns golden, add curry leaves. Stir, and add pigeon peas. Cook for 2-3 minutes.
- Add ground masala, stir and remove from heat.

TOPPU KARI - I

Spinach with Lentils

Serves: 3-4

¾ cup pigeon peas (toover or arhar dal)
¼ tsp turmeric powder
1 tsp coriander powder
Salt to taste
½ kg spinach (cleaned, picked and washed)
1 green chilli (slit and deseeded)
¼ fresh coconut (ground)

For tempering:

2 tbsp oil
¼ tsp mustard seeds
1" piece dried red chilli (deseeded)
2 cloves garlic (crushed)
1 onion (chopped)

- Wash dal and soak in water for 30 minutes.
- Boil dal in 2 cups water with turmeric powder for 30 minutes or till soft. Add coriander powder, salt, spinach and green chilli.
- Continue cooking on low heat till spinach is tender. Add ground coconut, stir and remove from heat.
- Heat oil for tempering in another pan, add mustard seeds and allow to splutter. Add red chilli and fry for a few seconds. Add garlic and when it turns golden, add onion. Fry till onion turns golden brown.

- Pour in cooked spinach. Stir and remove from heat.

Note: Several varieties of spinach can be used for this recipe, though the local variety called keerai grown in Kodagu is normally used.

TOPPU KARI-II

Dry Spinach Curry

Serves: 2

½ cup oil
2 onions (chopped)
½ kg spinach (cleaned, picked and washed)
2 green chillies (slit and deseeded)
Salt to taste

- Heat oil in pan and fry onions till golden. Add spinach, green chillies and salt and cook on low heat, stirring frequently till tender.

Note: No water is added to this dish while cooking.

Traditionally the local variety of spinach called keerai is used for this dish.

KAAD MAANGÉ

Wild Mango Curry

Serves: 2

¼ kg ripe wild mangoes
¼ tsp red chilli powder
1 tsp turmeric powder
Salt to taste
Jaggery syrup, made from 1½" piece jaggery dissolved in ½ cup water

Masala for grinding:

1 tsp coriander seeds
A pinch of fenugreek seeds (methi)
¼ tsp cumin seeds
¼ tsp mustard seeds

For tempering:

2 tbsp oil
¼ tsp mustard seeds
1-2 dried red chillies (deseeded)
2-3 cloves garlic (crushed)
1 onion (chopped)
3-4 curry leaves

- Heat a tava or griddle and add ingredients for masala to be ground, in the order given. Roast each ingredient for a few seconds before adding the next. Stir constantly to avoid burning. Cool and grind to a fine powder.

- Wash mangoes, remove stalks and cut into largish sections with skin, leaving stones intact. Put mangoes, including stone and skin, into a pan and mix with chilli powder, turmeric powder, ground masala and salt.
- In another pan, heat oil for tempering, add mustard seeds and allow to splutter. Put in red chilli, stir, add crushed garlic and stir. When garlic begins to colour, add chopped onions and curry leaves. Fry till onions turn golden.
- Add mango and masala mixture and stir for a few minutes. Add 2 cups water and cook mangoes till tender.
- Strain in jaggery syrup and cook till gravy thickens.

Note: Instead of cutting the mangoes, they may be peeled and added whole.

PACHCHADI

Vegetables in Spiced Curd

A curd-based recipe, pachchadi is usually served with palau or neyi koolu as a refreshing contrast to the heavy ghee and masala of the palau and ghee rice. However it can be eaten with plain boiled rice. It is made with cucumber, ripe tomatoes, ripe sweet mangoes (wild or cultivated), or fresh ginger.

CHOUTÉ PACHCHADI

Cucumber in Spiced Curd

Serves: 3-4

½ kg cucumber
1½ cups curd

Ground to a fine paste:

½ fresh coconut
1-2 green chillies
¼ tsp mustard seeds
4 cloves garlic
1 small bunch coriander leaves
Salt to taste

For tempering:

1½ tbsp oil
¼ tsp mustard seeds
2 dried red chillies (deseeded)

4-5 cloves garlic (crushed)
1 onion (chopped, optional)

- Peel cucumber if the skin is thick. Grate or chop fine.
- Mix with ground spices and curd.
- Heat oil for tempering in a pan and add mustard seeds. Allow to splutter and add red chillies and crushed garlic. When garlic turns golden, add onions, if used and fry till translucent. Pour into cucumber mixture.

Variation: **Kaad Maangé Pachchadi (Wild Mangoes in Spiced Curd)**
Use ½ kg ripe wild mangoes in place of cucumber. Peel and scrape off pulp from peel. Add scraped pulp and whole mangoes in place of cucumber.

Add jaggery syrup made with jaggery the size of a walnut or 2 tsp sugar, as even when ripe, wild mangoes tend to be sour.

The dish can also be made with cultivated ripe mangoes. However, no sweetening is required here and the skin and seeds should be discarded.

Tomato Pachchadi (Tomato in Spiced Curd)
Use ½ kg ripe tomatoes, cut into ½" cubes and add in place of cucumber. Tomatoes may be peeled, if desired. Pour boiling water over tomatoes. Leave for 5 minutes and plunge into cold water. The skins will come off easily.

INJI PACHCHADI

Ginger in Spiced Curd

Serves: 2-3

2 medium-sized onions (finely sliced in rings)
1 cup curd

For tempering:

1 tbsp oil
$\frac{1}{4}$ tsp mustard seeds
2 pieces dried red chillies (1" each, deseeded)
3-4 curry leaves

Ground to a fine paste:

$\frac{1}{2}$ fresh coconut
1" piece fresh ginger
1 tsp sugar
Salt to taste

- Heat oil for tempering in a pan and add mustard seeds. Allow to splutter. Add red chillies and curry leaves. Stir for a few seconds and add ground spices. Stir and remove quickly from heat. Add onions and curd and mix well.

Variation: **Pudina Pachchadi (Mint in Spiced Curd)**
Substitute 2-3 sprigs mint leaves in place of ginger.

KAIPULI PACHCHADI

Bitter Orange in Spiced Curd

Makes: 1-2 cups

The variety of oranges used for this dish have a hard, tough, green skin.

2 bitter oranges
1 cup curd

Ground to a fine paste:

½ fresh coconut (grated)
2 green chillies
4 cloves garlic
Salt to taste
1 tbsp sugar

Tempering:

½ tbsp oil
¼ tsp mustard seeds
2 pieces dried red chilli (1" each, deseeded)
2-3 cloves garlic (crushed)
3-4 curry leaves

- Peel oranges and remove pith and seeds.
- Mix orange flakes with ground spices.
- Heat oil for tempering in a pan, put in mustard seeds, allow to splutter and add red chillies. Fry for a few seconds and add crushed garlic and curry leaves. When garlic begins to colour add oranges, and stir.

Add curd, mix well and remove from heat.

- Serve with ghee rice or palau.

Note: Traditionally bitter oranges are first roasted in hot coals till the rind is cooked black. Roasting gives the dish a better flavour.

Chutneys and Pickles

CHUTNEYS

In Kodagu a variety of chutneys are eaten with akki otti or dosai, at breakfast.

ELLU PAJJI

Sesame Seed Chutney

Makes: 1 cup

2 tbsp sesame seeds (til), dry roasted
½ fresh coconut (grated)
3 green or red chillies (deseeded)
Tamarind (without seeds or fibre), the size of a marble
Salt to taste

- Grind all ingredients together to a smooth, stiff paste, adding a very little water if necessary.
- Serve with akki otti or dosai and ghee ōr butter.

INJI PAJJI

Ginger Chutney

Makes: 1 cup

2 onions (finely sliced in rings)

Ground to a fine paste:

½ fresh coconut (grated)
1" piece ginger
1 tsp sugar
1 tsp thick tamarind paste
Salt to taste

For tempering:

1 tbsp oil
¼ tsp mustard seeds
2 dried red chillies (1" each, deseeded)
3-4 curry leaves

- Heat oil for tempering in a pan. Add mustard seeds and allow to splutter. Add red chillies and curry leaves. Remove from heat and mix in ground masala. Add onions to chutney.
- Mix well and serve.

KEMBU PAJJI

Colocasia Chutney

You need very tender colocasia leaves which have not yet opened, for this chutney.

A handful of tender, unfurled colocasia leaves
1 medium sized, but not thick colocasia leaf
Salt to taste
1 green chilli (deseeded, optional)
3-4 cloves garlic
Juice of a small lime

For tempering:

1 tbsp oil
¼ tsp mustard seeds
1" piece dried red chilli (deseeded)
2-3 cloves garlic, crushed
3-4 curry leaves
1 medium-sized onion, finely chopped (optional)

- Wash colocasia leaves.
- Wrap tender leaves in the large leaf, and roast buried in hot ashes under hot coals. You could use an oven as a substitute.
- When the tender leaves are cooked—about 5-10 minutes, unwrap them.
- Mix with salt, green chilli and garlic. Grind to a smooth paste, adding a few drops of water if necessary.

- Heat oil for tempering in a pan, add mustard seeds and allow to splutter. Add red chilli and fry for a few seconds. Add crushed garlic. When garlic begins to turn gold, add curry leaves and chopped onion. Fry till onion is translucent.
- Add colocasia leaf paste, stir, remove from heat and add lime juice.

Note: The lime juice, in addition to enhancing the flavour, prevents itching in the mouth, which is sometimes caused by colocasia leaves.

MUDARÉ PAJJI

Horse gram Chutney

Makes: 1 cup

3 tbsp dry roasted horse gram (kulthi ka dal)
½ fresh coconut (grated)
4 dried red chillies (deseeded)
Tamarind the size of a marble (without seeds or fibre)
Salt to taste

- Grind all ingredients into a smooth paste, adding a very little water if necessary.
- The chutney should be thick.

PULINJEPULI PAJJI-I

Tamarind Chutney

Makes: 2 cups

¼ kg tamarind
2-3 pieces jaggery (1" cubes)
Salt to taste
1 large dried red chilli (deseeded)
¼" piece ginger
2 tbsp oil
1 tbsp groundnuts

- Soak tamarind and jaggery separately in one cup water each for 30 minutes. Extract tamarind pulp and strain through a piece of muslin. Strain in jaggery syrup. Add salt, red chilli and ginger and grind to a smooth paste.
- Heat oil in a pan, add groundnuts and fry for one minute. Add tamarind paste and simmer on low heat till mixture begins to leave sides of pan. Cool and store in a glass jar.
- Serve with akki otti or dosai and butter or ghee.

Variation: One finely sliced onion may be used instead of groundnuts..

PULINJEPULI PAJJI-II

Tamarind Chutney

Makes: 1-1½ cups

1 lime-sized ball of tamarind
100 gm jaggery
Salt to taste

Masala:

1 tsp fenugreek seeds (methi)
1 tsp cumin seeds
1 tsp mustard seeds

- Soak tamarind in one cup water and squeeze out pulp and strain into a pan.
- Dissolve jaggery in one cup water and strain into tamarind pulp.
- Heat a tava or griddle and dry roast masala ingredients in the order given. Roast each ingredient for a few seconds before adding next. Stir continuously and take care the spices do not burn. Cool and grind fine.
- Add ground masala and salt to tamarind and jaggery mixture. Stir well and simmer for 10 minutes or until mixture begins to leave sides of pan.

TENGÉ PAJJI

Coconut Chutney

Makes: 1-2 cups

1 fresh coconut (grated)
1" piece tamarind (without seeds or fibre)
4 green chillies (deseeded)
Salt to taste
1 small bunch coriander leaves
A pinch of fenugreek seeds (methi)

- Grind all ingredients together.
- Serve with akki otti or dosai and ghee or butter.

PICKLES

Great care is needed while making pickles. Vessels and containers for storing them must be clean and dry. Hands must also be dry or else the pickle will spoil.

CHORENGÉ PARA

Lime Pickle

12 ripe limes
1 cup rock salt
15 green chillies, or to taste (optional)
1 pod garlic (optional)

Ground to a fine paste:

20 dried red chillies
1 tbsp mustard seeds
3 pods garlic, peeled
A little lime juice or malt vinegar

- Wash and dry limes. Cut each lime in 4 and remove seeds. Place limes and a little rock salt in a pan and dry roast lightly on low heat.
- Put a thin layer of rock salt in a ceramic container. Put a layer of limes over it, topped by a layer of rock salt. Repeat procedure till the top is covered with a layer of salt.
- Leave for ten days, and stir every 2 days.

- After ten days, add ground spices and mix well.
- If green chillies are being used, wash and thoroughly dry chillies. Add to pickle.
- If garlic is being used clean and leave cloves whole. Add to pickle.
- Mix well and cover with a tight lid.
- The pickle will be ready for use after 2-3 weeks.

Note: Do not use water and keep hands dry while grinding spices for the pickle.

KAAD MAANGÉ PARA

Wild Mango Pickle

This requires tender green wild mangoes before the stones begin to harden. The skin of the mangoes should be whole and the stalks should not be cut too close to the skin. Usually the green mangoes are collected in the season, and preserved in brine for later use.

1 kg green mangoes
½ kg salt
½ kg dried red chillies
¼ kg mustard seeds

- Wash mangoes and place in an earthenware or ceramic container. Add just enough water to cover. Retain this water. Remove mangoes and dry with a clean cloth.
- Put reserved water into a pan. Add salt, and bring to boil. Cool.
- Put mangoes in boiled salt water and allow to soak for 4-5 days.
- Grind red chilli and mustard seeds to a fine paste, using some of the boiled salted water if necessary.
- Remove mangoes from water, mix with ground spices, and store in a ceramic jar. Cover with lid and tie a clean cloth tightly round the top.

- There will be a small quantity of the salty liquid resulting from the wet mangoes, in the mixture.
- Once the spice mixture is absorbed, the pickle is ready. This will take about 3-4 days.

KOYILÉ MEEN PARA

Paddy-field Fish Pickle

This pickle is made with the small paddy-field fish available in Kodagu. You could use any other small fish.

250 gm paddy-field or any other small fish
¼ cup white vinegar
1 cup oil

Ground to a fine paste:

4 cloves garlic, peeled
3 dried red chillies (deseeded)
A pinch of fenugreek seeds (methi)
1 tsp salt
½ tsp mustard seeds
2 cloves

- Clean fish by washing with water and a little extra vinegar, or vinegar with salt. Rinse out with fresh water.
- In a pan heat oil, add fish and fry on low heat till it begins to turn brown. Remove fish from oil, without breaking, and put aside.
- To the same oil, add ground spices and fry on low heat, stirring constantly, till mixture becomes dry.
- Add fried fish, mix well, fry for a minute and remove from heat.

- Add ¼ cup vinegar and mix well. Cool and store in a glass jar.
- There should be half inch layer of oil over the pickle. If there is not enough, heat a little more oil and pour over pickle.

ONNAK MEEN PARA

Pickled dried fish

Choose a good, fleshy variety of salted dried fish for this pickle.

½ kg salted dried fish, cut into 1" pieces
750 + 200 ml white vinegar
400 ml oil
10 green chillies (deseeded and finely chopped)
1" piece ginger (finely chopped)
1 pod garlic (finely chopped)

Ground to a fine paste:

2 pod garlic (cleaned)
1 tsp chilli powder
3 cloves
3 pieces cinnamon (1" each)
A pinch of asafoetida (hing)
1 tsp fenugreek seeds (methi)
1" piece ginger
50 ml white vinegar

- Soak salted fish in 750 ml vinegar for 2-3 hours. The fish should be covered by vinegar, and after soaking, the salt in the fish should have been absorbed by it. Wash fish pieces in the same vinegar, squeeze and put aside. Discard vinegar.
- Heat half the oil in a pan, add fish and fry till it turns

light brown. Remove from oil, and keep aside. Discard oil.

- Put remaining oil, in a pan, add green chillies, ginger, and garlic and fry for one minute on low heat till they give out an aroma. Add ground masala and continue frying for further 1-2 minutes.
- Add fish and fry for 2-3 minutes. Remove from heat, add 200 ml vinegar and mix well.
- Cool and store in a glass or ceramic jar.

PANDI YERCHI PARA

Pork Pickle

¼ kg pork
1½ tsp salt
¼ tsp turmeric powder
1 cup oil
¼ cup white vinegar

Ground to a fine paste:
4 dried red chillies (de-seeded)
6 large cloves garlic
½" piece ginger
A pinch of fenugreek seeds (methi)
¼ tsp mustard seeds
¼ cup white vinegar

- Wash and cut pork into ½"-¾" pieces. Mix with salt and turmeric powder and steam in a pressure cooker. Do not add any water to the pork.
- Remove any liquid that may be in the pressure cooker with the pork.
- Heat oil in a pan, add steamed pork and cook till pork is dry. Remove pork from oil and set aside.
- Add ground spices to pan and fry till masala dries. Add cooked pork and fry for 5 minutes. Remove from heat and add vinegar. There should be a half-inch layer of oil covering the pickle.
- Cool and store in a glass jar.

Desserts and Snacks

ALBAI

Rice and Coconut Dessert

½ kg sannakki or basmati rice
1 fresh coconut (grated)
Muslin cloth
3 cups sugar

- Wash rice and soak for 2-3 hours. Drain and grind to a very smooth paste with grated coconut, adding a little water while grinding. The mixture should be of thin pouring consistency.
- Strain into a pan through a muslin cloth, add sugar and mix well.
- Place pan on high heat and cook, stirring constantly till it begins to thicken. Lower heat and cook till mixture thickens further, and begins to leave sides of pan.
- Pour on to a greased thali or plate. Flatten and smoothen top. When cool, cut into diamonds and serve.

BADAAMI PAALU

Almond Milk

Serves: 6-8

150 gm almonds (blanched and peeled)
1½ litres milk
1 cup sugar
Powdered seeds of 3-4 green cardamoms
A small pinch of saffron soaked in 2 tbsp warm milk

- Grind almonds to a fine paste.
- Boil milk for about 20 minutes till it thickens slightly. Add sugar and ground almonds. Boil mixture till you smell the aroma of almonds. Add cardamom and saffron and boil for a further 3-5 minutes.
- Remove from heat, cool and serve.
- It should be of drinking consistency.

BADUVA KAJJAAYA

Rice and Jaggery Cakes

1 kg sannakki or basmati rice
1 kg jaggery
Oil for deep frying

- Wash and soak rice in water for 12 hours. Drain completely. Pound rice to a smooth powder and sieve it to remove coarse bits.
- Dissolve jaggery in enough water to make a thick syrup, so that a drop put in water forms a lump and floats on the surface. It should not immediately dissolve in the water. Strain syrup.
- Mix powdered rice with jaggery syrup and cook, stirring continuously till it reaches the consistency of a dough.
- Flatten small balls of dough on a piece of damp cloth into a disc about ¼" thick and 2" to 3" in diameter. Punch a hole in the middle of each disc with your finger.
- Heat oil in a kadahi or deep frying pan and deep-fry the discs. Serve as a teatime snack.

BERAMBUTTU

Jaggery and Rice Flour Dessert

Serves: 3-4

1 cup rice flour (made of parboiled rice roasted to a golden brown colour and powdered)
⅓ kg jaggery
¼ tsp salt
Powdered seeds of 1-2 green cardamoms
½ cup sesame seeds (til), dry roasted
½ fresh coconut (grated)
½ cup ghee

- Boil 2 cups water and add jaggery. Stir to dissolve and make a syrup. Strain into a pan, and cool.
- Add rice flour, cardamom seeds and salt and mix well. Place pan on low heat and cook till thick and water is absorbed.
- Put berambuttu in a dish and serve with sesame seeds, grated coconut and melted ghee placed in separate bowls.

BOODI KUMBALA HALVA

Ash Gourd Halva

1 kg ash gourd (petha), peeled and cut upto 2" cubes
Sugar equal in volume to ash gourd purée
1 cup ghee
Powdered seeds of 3 green cardamoms
10 cashewnuts (chopped)
Red food colour mixed in 1 tbsp milk (optional)

- Pressure-cook ash gourd till very soft. Purée ash gourd and pour into a thick-bottomed pan with an equal volume of sugar.
- Stir and place pan on heat. Continue stirring and cooking till sugar is completely dissolved and ash gourd turns brown.
- Gradually add ghee in small quantities and keep stirring till ghee begins to separate.
- Add cashewnuts, powdered cardamom and red coloring (if desired). Mix well.
- Pour halva onto a greased thali or plate, flatten and smoothen out top. Cut into diamonds when cool.

CHIKKALUNDÉ

Popped Rice Sweet

In Kodagu, traditionally rice was 'popped' by roasting unhusked rice in the same way as popcorn is made. Popcorn or puffed rice, coarsely, crushed may be used as an alternative.

2 cups popped rice
½ cup sesame seeds (til), dry roasted
½ fresh coconut (grated)
A pinch of salt
½ cup thick jaggery syrup
Oil for deep frying

Batter:

½ cup rice flour
¼ tsp turmeric powder
A pinch of salt

- Mix popped rice, sesame seeds, coconut, salt and jaggery.
- Make a thin batter of rice flour, water, turmeric powder and salt.
- Make lime-sized balls of popped rice mixture, dip in prepared batter and deep fry in oil.

GINNU

Sweet Cheese

This is made from the first and second day milk of a cow after she has calved.

1 litre milk
2 cups sugar
Powdered seeds of 4-5 green cardamoms

- Add sugar and cardamom powder to milk. Pour mixture into the top of a double boiler and cook till milk solidifies.
- Spread on a greased thali or plate, smoothen out top. Cut into diamonds and serve.

HOLIGÉ

Stuffed Bengal Gram Cakes

¼ kg Bengal gram (channa dal)
½ coconut (ground, optional)
¼ kg jaggery
Powdered seeds of 3-4 green cardamoms
1 kg flour (maida)
¼ tsp turmeric powder (optional)
¼ tsp salt
1 cup + 1 tbsp oil
8" piece of banana leaf or plastic sheet

- Wash dal and place in a pan with 2 cups water. Place pan on heat, bring to boil, lower heat and cook till soft adding more water if necessary.
- Add coconut, jaggery, and cardamom powder. Mix well and remove from heat. If mixture is moist, continue cooking on low heat to remove excess moisture.
- Mix flour with one cup water, turmeric powder and salt. Add one cup oil, and knead to make a very soft dough.
- Soften banana leaf over a flame, and rub one tablespoon oil over it.
- Pinch off a lemon sized piece of dough, place on banana leaf and flatten into a disc. Pinch off a lime sized piece of dal mixture and place on flattened

dough. Bring edges of dough together, to enclose filling, flatten and roll into a 6" disc on the banana leaf.

- Heat a tava or griddle, place flattened cake on tava and cook on both sides.
- Make remaining cakes in the same way.

Variation: Pigeon peas (toover or arhar dal) may be used instead of Bengal gram and jaggery may be substituted with sugar.

KARJIKAI - I

Sweet Puffs

2 cups flour (maida)
2 tsp cornflour (optional)
2 tbsp ghee
2 cups fresh coconut (grated and lightly roasted to dry)
$1\frac{1}{2}$ cups sugar
$1\frac{1}{2}$ cups sesame (til) or poppy seeds (khus khus), dry roasted
Powdered seeds of 2 green cardamoms
Oil for deep frying

- Mix flour and cornflour with ghee and a little water. Knead well to make a soft dough. Set aside and cover with a moist cloth.
- Mix coconut, sugar, sesame or poppy seeds, and cardamom powder together.
- Pinch off a lime-sized ball of dough and role out into a flat round about 4" in diameter. Place some of the coconut mixture on one side of dough. Fold over other half to make a half-moon shape and seal edges with finger tips or a roller-cutter. Make remaining puffs in the same way.
- Deep-fry in oil.

Note: Cornflour makes the puffs softer and crisper.

AKKI PAAYASA

Rice and Milk Dessert

Serves: 5-6

Paayasa is served at the end of a meal and sometimes with ripe bananas.

1 cup Bengal gram (channa dal)
1 cup sannakki or basmati rice
4-5 green cardamoms (whole)
⅓ kg jaggery
1 cup coconut milk (extracted from 1 coconut)
1 tbsp ghee
½ cup cashewnuts
½ cup sultanas (kishmish)

- Wash and soak Bengal gram overnight in 5 cups water, to soften so that it cooks at the same time as rice.
- Put gram in a pan with soaking water and bring to boil. Add rice, bring to boil, lower heat and cook for about 10 minutes. Add cardamoms and cook on low heat till rice and gram are tender.
- Dissolve jaggery in one cup water. Strain jaggery syrup and add with coconut milk into rice-gram mixture.
- Heat ghee, and fry cashewnuts lightly, add sultanas, fry for a few seconds and add to paayasa. The paayasa should not be too thick.

KHUSKHUSÉ PAAYASA

Poppy Seed Dessert

Serves: 4-5

1 cup poppy seeds (khus khus)
½ cup sannakki or basmati rice
1 fresh coconut (grated)
1 cup sugar
1 tbsp ghee
1 tbsp sultanas (kishmish)
10-12 almonds (blanched and slivered)
Powdered seeds of 3-4 green cardamoms
A small pinch of saffron (soaked in 2 tbsp warm milk)
1 cup milk
Muslin cloth

- Soak rice and poppy seeds separately for about three hours.
- Drain and grind together with grated coconut to a fine paste, adding water gradually until the mixture is of pouring consistency. Strain through a piece of muslin and add sugar.
- Heat ghee and fry almonds and sultanas lightly. Add to rice-poppy seed mixture with ghee. Add cardamom powder, saffron and milk, and cook on low heat, stirring constantly till mixture thickens.
- The paayasa, when ready, should be of pouring consistency.

SEMIGÉ PAAYASA

Vermicelli and Milk Dessert

Serves: 4-5

2 cups vermicelli
1+1 tbsp ghee
2 cups milk
1-1½ cups sugar
2 tbsp cashewnuts
2 tbsp sultanas (kishmish)

- Lightly fry vermicelli in one tablespoon ghee. Add 2 cups water and cook till soft but not dark in colour. Add milk and sugar.
- Heat remaining ghee, fry cashewnuts, followed by sultanas, lightly.
- Mix with paayasa and serve.

HESRU PAAYASA

Green Bean Dessert

Serves: 3-4

1 cup whole green beans (sabut mung)
3-4 green cardamoms
1 heaped tbsp sugar
1 tbsp sultanas (kishmish)
1 tbsp grated coconut

- Wash dal and soak overnight in 2 cups water.
- Place dal and water in which it was soaked in a pan with cardamoms and bring to boil. Lower heat and cook till done. Add more water if required. It should have a thick pouring consistency.
- Add sugar and sultana. Stir till sugar is dissolved.
- Stir in grated coconut and serve.

Note: When this dish is made with split green beans (chhilke ki mung ki dal) it is only ever served on the eleventh day ceremony after death. It is never prepared on any other day in a Kodava home. The split dal does not need to be soaked. It should be lightly dry roasted before boiling.

KULURU PUTTU

Rice and Coconut Sweet

200 gm rice
1 cup fresh coconut (grated)
200 gm sugar
½ tsp powdered green cardamom seeds
2 tbsp ghee
Pinch of salt

- Wash rice and soak in water for one hour. Drain, add grated coconut and grind to a smooth paste.
- Put paste into a heavy bottomed pan, add 6 cups water, sugar, cardamom powder, ghee and salt.
- Cook on low heat, allowing mixture to boil, stirring continuously to prevent it from sticking to pan or forming lumps. When mixture starts leaving sides of pan, remove from heat and pour onto a greased thali or plate. Smoothen out top.
- When cool, cut into diamonds and serve.

RAVÉ UNDAY

Semolina Sweet

1½ cups + 1 tbsp ghee
5-6 cloves
½ kg fine semolina
Powdered seeds of 3 green cardamom
1½-2 cups sugar
½ cup cashewnuts (chopped)
½ cup sultanas (kishmish)
½ cup milk
1 dry coconut (kopra), grated

- Heat 1½ cups ghee in a pan on low heat. Put in cloves, stir for a few seconds, add semolina and fry to a pale brown colour. Add cardamom powder and remove from heat.
- Boil sugar with one cup water to make a syrup and add to semolina mixture.
- Heat one tablespoon ghee in a pan and lightly fry cashew nuts and sultanas. Add to semolina. Mix well.
- Shape into lime-sized balls while mixture is still warm. If mixture is too dry, sprinkle a little milk on it.

Note: Ravé Unday is a dry sweet that can be stored and served at tea time.

ELLU PAAKA

Sesame Seed Sweet

This is a special dish given to a new mother. From the thirteenth to fortieth day after delivery, the mother is given one cup of ellu paaka every morning on an empty stomach in order to 'cool' the system.

1 kg sesame seeds (til), dry roasted and coarsely ground
4 fresh coconuts, grated
¼ kg fenugreek seeds (methi), dry roasted and coarsely ground
1 kg jaggery
½ kg ghee
Cold water (enough to cover jaggery)

- Add one litre hot water to grated coconut and leave aside for 15 minutes. Squeeze out thick coconut milk.
- Add 2 litres hot water to coconut, and extract second lot of coconut milk, which will be thin.
- Place jaggery in a pan. Pour enough water to cover. Heat to dissolve.
- Put thin coconut milk into a pan and place on heat. Bring to boil, add sesame seed and fenugreek powder, and stir.
- Strain jaggery syrup into mixture.
- Continue cooking and stirring till mixture is nearly dry.

- Add thick coconut milk, cook and stir for a minute. Add ghee and mix well.
- Cool and store in a glass or ceramic jar.

BAALÉ MURUKU

Banana Sweet

In Kodagu the Mara baalé variety of bananas is used for this dish. You can use any type of soft, moist banana.

10 ripe Mara baalé or green skinned sweet bananas
¼ cup rice flour
¾ cup flour (maida)
½ tsp powdered green cardamom seeds
1 tbsp fresh grated coconut (optional)
¼ tsp salt
2 tsp sugar (optional)
Oil for deep frying

- Mash bananas to a smooth pulp. Add rice flour, flour, cardamom powder, grated coconut, salt and sugar. Mix and knead to make a soft dough. It should be of dropping consistency.
- Heat oil in a kadahi or deep frying pan.
- Shape dough into balls slightly smaller in size than an egg and fry till they are a brown colour. Remove with a serated flat spoon or skimmer.

THAMBUTTU

Banana Sweet

Serves: 6-8

This dish is specially prepared during Puththari, the harvest festival. It requires rice flour made of parboiled rice which is dry roasted till golden and powdered.

10 ripe Maré baalé or green skinned sweet bananas
1 cup rice flour made as above
1 tsp fenugreek seeds (methi), powdered
Powdered seeds of 1-2 green cardamoms
1 tsp sugar
1 tsp salt
1 cup ghee (melted)
½ fresh coconut (grated)
1 cup sesame seeds (til), lightly dry roasted

- Mash bananas to a very smooth paste, add rice flour, powdered cardamom, fenugreek, sugar and salt. Mix well. The mixture should be firm, but soft.
- Place mixture on a plate and serve with ghee, grated coconut and sesame seeds in separate bowls.
- The banana mixture is taken in individual plates, a small well is made in the centre and the accompaniments are placed in the well and then eaten.

Note: Thambuttu is always freshly prepared as the bananas tend to get discoloured.

FRIED NOOLPUTTU

Fried String Hoppers

- Leftover noolputtu can be sun-dried and stored in an airtight tin. When required it can be deep-fried and sprinkled with fresh grated coconut and sugar and served as a tea-time snack.

KOOVALÉ PUTTU-I

Banana and Rice Sweet

This was traditionally steamed in leaves of koovalé plants found in the jungles of Kodagu, which have a distinctive fragrance. Since these are not easily available, banana leaves may be used.

10 ripe bananas (mara baalé or green skinned sweet bananas)
1½ cups broken rice (slightly bigger than semolina grains)
1 tbsp jaggery or sugar or to taste
½ fresh coconut, grated or finely chopped
A pinch of bicarbonate of soda
Banana leaves (cut into 6-8" squares and gently wilted over fire)

- Mash bananas into a very smooth paste. Mix all ingredients except banana leaves and set aside for about one hour, to let rice absorb the moisture. The mixture should not be too thick as there has to be enough moisture for the rice to cook.
- Put 2 or 3 tbsp of mixture in the centre of each piece of banana leaf, and fold into rectangular packets.
- Steam in a chekala or steamer till they are firm.

Note: To wilt, or soften banana leaves, gently pass the leaf over a live flame, ensuring that every part of the leaf has been softened.

KOOVALÉ PUTTU-II

Rice and Jackfruit Sweet

The jack fruit used for this is a very juicy Kodagu variety which has a fibrous flesh that is not very suitable for serving at table.

1 cup broken rice (slightly larger than semolina grains)
Strained jack fruit juice to make a thick batter
Powdered seeds of 2-3 green cardamoms
¼ fresh coconut, finely chopped
Banana leaves (8" pieces, wilted over fire)

- Mix broken rice and jack fruit juice to make a thick but not stiff mixture. If a small quantity of it is placed on a flat surface it should level down. Add cardamom powder and coconut.
- In the centre of each banana leaf place mixture to cover an area of about 2" by 4". Fold leaf to make small rectangular packets. Put the packets in a chekala or steamer and steam till cooked and firm.

Note: To wilt, or soften banana leaves, gently pass the leaf over a live flame, ensuring that every part of the leaf has been softened.

CHAKKULI - I

Semolina and Rice Savouries

Special chakkuli moulds are used to press out the batter to make chakkuli. You may use a forcing bag with a star shaped nozzle instead.

1 cup semolina
1 cup rice flour
2 tbsp butter
1 tbsp sugar
1 tbsp cumin or sesame seeds (til)
Oil for deep frying

- Put semolina and 3 cups water in a pan and cook till soft. Add rice flour and cook till it reaches the consistency of medium thick dough. Add butter, sugar and cumin or sesame seeds and mix well.
- Use a chakkuli mould to press batter on to a wet clean cloth or a piece of banana leaf in concentric circles, to form a disc about 3" in diameter.
- Alternately, put batter into a forcing bag with a star shaped nozzle and force out batter.
- Deep fry on low heat.

CHAKKULI - II

Rice and Gram Flour Savouries

½ cup cooked rice
½ cup rice flour
1 cup gram flour made from roasted gram
1 tsp cumin seeds
½ tsp red chilli powder
2 tbsp butter
Salt to taste
Oil for deep frying

- Mix all ingredients, except oil, to make a soft dough.
- Use a chakkuli mould to make small, two spiral rounds about 3" in diameter on a flat surface (damp cloth or banana leaf).
- Alternately use a forcing bag and star shaped nozzle.
- Deep-fry in hot oil.

Note: The gram used for making this dish is the roasted eating variety. The gram is called hurigadale in Karnataka.

KARJIKAI - II
Mince Puffs

2 cups flour (maida)
2 tsp cornflour (optional)
2 tbsp ghee
¾ kg minced mutton
½ tsp turmeric powder
¼ tsp red chilli powder
1 tsp coriander powder
½ tsp cumin powder
1 green chilli (finely chopped)
½" piece ginger (finely chopped)
½ cup shelled green peas
Oil for deep frying

For tempering:

2 tbsp oil
4-5 gloves garlic (crushed)
1 medium-sized onion (finely chopped)

- Mix flour, cornflour, ghee and a little water to make a soft dough. Cover with a wet cloth and set aside.
- Cook mutton with next 6 ingrediens and a little water till done.
- Heat oil for tempering and add crushed garlic. When it begins to turn golden add onion. Fry till onion begins to turn golden brown. Add cooked minced meat and shelled green peas, and continue

cooking on low heat till green peas are cooked and excess water is dried out.

- Make lime-sized balls of the dough and roll out into flat rounds about 4" in diameter. Place some mince on one side and fold to make a half-moon. Seal edges with finger tips or a roller-cutter.
- Deep fry in oil.

BONDU

Baby's First Solid

½ cup cooked rice

¼ cup thick curd (obtained by hanging curd in a clean cloth to drain out whey)

1 tbsp fresh cream (top of cow's milk)

- Grind all ingredients to a smooth paste and feed it to the baby.
- The rice should be cooked very soft and curd should not be sour.

Glossary

English	Hindi	Kodava
Almond	Badam	Badami
Asafoetida	Hing	Ing
Ash gourd	Petha	Boodi Kumbala
Aubergine	Baigan	Bainé
Bamboo shoot	Bans ki kalli	Baimalé
Banana	Kela	Baalé
Bengal gram	Channa dal	Kadalé bélé
Bitter gourd	Karela	Kaipekké
Bitter Orange	—	Kaipuli
Urad		
– whole	Urad	Uddhu
– husked	Dhuli urad ki dal	Uddhu bélé
Black peppercorn	Kali mirch	Nallamalu
Black-eyed beans	Lobia	Tadugini
Bottle gourd	Ghia/loki	Torai
Butter	Makhan	Bonne nei

English	Hindi	Kodava
Cardamom		
– green	Hari elaichi	Yelakki
Cashewnut	Kajoo	Gerubeeja
Chicken	Murgh	Koli
Chilli	Mirchi	Malu
– dried red	Sookhi mirch	Chonda malu
– green	Hari mirch	Pachai malu
– powder	Lal mirch	Malu podi
Cinnamon	Dal cheeni	Pattay
Clarified butter	Ghee	Urku neyi
Cloves	Laung	Lavanga
Coconut		
– dry	Kopra	Kopri
– fresh	Nariyal	Tenge
– milk	Nariyal ka doodh	Tengepalu
Colocasia	Arvi	Kembu
– leaves	Arvi patta	Kembu toppu
Coriander		
– fresh	Kothmir	Sambara toppu
–seeds	Dhania	Sambara
Cream	Malai	Péré
Cucumber	Kheera	Chouté
Cumin seeds	Jheera	Jeerigé
Curd	Dahi	Katti moru
Curry leaves	Curry patta	Kodanari toppu
Drumsticks	Surjan ki phali	Nuggekai
Fenugreek seeds	Methi dana	Menté kal

English	Hindi	Kodava
Fish	Machchi	Meen
Flour		
– refined	Maida	Merkin podi
French bean seeds	Farash binis beej	Chettu kuru
French beans	Farash binis	Chettu
Garlic	Lahsun	Bollulli
Ginger	Adrak	Inji
Green peas	Mattar	Paché bataani
Groundnut	Mungphali	Nela kadalay
Horse gram	Kulthi ka dal	Mudaré
Jackfruit	Kathal	Chekké
Jaggery	Gur	Bella
Knol kohl	Ganth gobi	Noo kol
Lime	Limbu	Chorengé
Mangalore cucumber	—	Bollari
Mango		
– cultivated	Aam	Maangé
– wild	—	Kaad maangé
Milk	Doodh	Paalu
Mint	Phudina	Pudina
Mushroom	Guchchi	Kummu
Mustard seeds	Sarson	Kadu
Mutton		
– goat	Gosht	Aadu yerchi
– sheep	Gosht	Kori yerchi
Oil	Tel	Enne

English	Hindi	Kodava
Onion	Pyaz	Eeruli
Paddy-field fish	—	Koyilé meen
Pigeon peas	Toover/Arhar	Tori bélé
Poppy seeds	Khus khus	Khuskhusé
Pork	Suvar ka gosht	Pandi yerchi
Potato	Aloo	Vilati kandé
Prawn	Jhinga	Chatté meen
Pumpkin		
– white	Seetaphul/ kaddu	Kai kumbala
– yellow	Seetaphul/ kaddu	Kumbala
Radish – white	Safed mooli	Moolangi
Rice		
– broken	Tukra chaval	Tari
– cooked	Chaval	Koolu
– flour	Chaval ka atta	Akki podi
– parboiled	Sela	Pukalakki
– popped	—	Koli poriakki
– uncooked	Chaval	Akki
Ridged gourd	Toorai	Keeré
Saffron	Kesar	Kum kum kesari
Salt	Namak	Uppu
Semolina	Sooji	Ravé
Sesame seeds	Til	Ellu
Snake gourd	Chirchinda	Padavala kai
Spinach	Palak	Keeré toppu
Sugar	Cheeni	Sakkaré
Sultana	Kishmish	Drakshé

English	Hindi	Kodava
Tamarind	Imli	Pulunji puli
Tomato	Tamatar	Tomato
Turmeric	Haldi	Manjé
Vermicelli	Sevian	Semigé

INDEX